D1519350

4

THE CAMEO SERIES

GRACE LIVINGSTON HILL

Tyndale House
Publishers, Inc.
Wheaton, Illinois

First printing, August 1984

Library of Congress Catalog Card Number 84-50538
ISBN 0-8423-1477-6, cloth

Printed in the United States of America

CONTENTS

THE HOUSE ACROSS THE HEDGE

MIRIAM, humming a happy little tune, hurried about her morning tasks, washing the dishes, shaking out the cloth and folding it carefully, sweeping the hearth and the front door stone.

Occasionally, with glad anticipation in her eyes, she glanced out of the lattice to the house across the hedge; the hedge which separated her father's yard from the handsome grounds of the rich, influential Egyptian whose daughter Zelda was Miriam's dearest friend.

That hedge was also the dividing line between Goshen, where Miriam lived, and great, alluring, glittering Egypt where Zelda lived; but a hard-beaten path ran from door to door, and a distinct space in the hedge showed where the children of both houses had been wont to go back and forth from babyhood.

Miriam turned from gazing out the lattice as her

mother came in from the garden with a basket of herbs.

"Mother," she said eagerly, "I've finished everything now and I'd like to go over to Zelda's right away. She's giving a party tonight, Mother. A wonderful party. And she's invited Joseph and me. She wanted us to come over this morning and help her prepare."

Miriam's eyes shone like two dark stars. Her mother watched her with growing dismay as she put down her basket. "Oh, I'm sorry, dear," she said gently, "but you two mustn't be away from the house today!"

A stormy look came into Miriam's eyes. "Oh, but Mother, you don't understand! I must go. This isn't just an ordinary party. It's a dance, and there is to be an orchestra from the city, and caterers. A great many people are invited, the sons and daughters of officers high in authority. It is a great honor that we are invited. And you needn't worry about having to get me a new dress to wear. Zelda is going to lend me a lovely new one of her own, green and gold with crimson threads in the border. It just fits me and I look wonderful in it. There is a gold chain, and armlets and anklets of gold to wear with it, and Balthazar is getting me flowers from a real florist's to wear in my hair. He said, 'You will be the prettiest girl at my sister's party.' He has asked me to dance with him. Really, Mother, don't you see I must go? And Zelda's father has been so kind to my father, putting him into a better position. It wouldn't do to offend them."

"Miriam, I'm so sorry, dear child!" said her mother steadily. "But we are having a solemn feast tonight. God has commanded it. And you will have to be here!"

"Oh, Mother!" cried Miriam in desperation. "Why do we have such a tiresome, solemn old religion? I wish we had a religion like Zelda's. I went with her to the temple once. There was music and laughter, and dancing and flowers. Mother, why would I have to be here at the feast? Nobody would miss me if I stayed away."

"God would miss you!" said her mother seriously. "Listen, Miriam, we are going on a journey tonight! There is much to be done. It will take every minute to get ready."

"Oh, Mother! You've been talking about that journey a long time but we haven't gone yet. Why do you think we are going tonight? Zelda's father says that Pharaoh never intends to let us go, and he is close to the throne and ought to know. But anyway, even if we were allowed, Mother—why do *we* have to go with Israel? What do we want with a promised land? Why can't we stay right here? We have a nice home, and Zelda's father would always see that Father had a good place. He might even get something to do in the palace. Why can't we stay and be Egyptians, and take the Egyptian gods for ours? I'd like that so much better, Mother!"

"Stop, Miriam!" said her mother sharply. "You are speaking blasphemies. Don't you know that our God is greater than all gods, that he is the *only true* God? Oh, my child! I have sinned! We were told to keep our children separate from all other peoples lest they forget their God who has covenanted with them. We are a chosen generation, a royal people! We should not mingle with the world. And I have let you grow up in close companionship with these Egyptian children! That of which we were warned has come to pass! My child is wanting to leave her God to serve those who are not gods at all! Oh, I have sinned!" she sobbed. "I thought there was no harm while you were little children, and you begged so hard to play with them! You were so little! I thought when you grew up you would learn to understand!" She lifted her tear-wet eyes and spoke earnestly. "Miriam, you must never speak this way again. It is sin!"

Miriam stood sullenly with downcast countenance, still looking out the window toward Egypt.

"Well, anyhow, Joseph is going!" she pouted. "I heard him tell Zelda he would be over early to help Balthazar. They are going to the woods to get flowers to deck the house. And if Joseph goes I don't see why I can't go. He is only a year older than I am!"

The mother gave her a frightened look.

"He must not!" she said. "You don't understand. He must help your father all day. And he must not be away from the house tonight! There is danger outside of our door."

Miriam gave her mother a quick, startled look. "What do you mean—danger?"

Her mother faced her earnestly, sadly. "My dear, I haven't told you yet. I dreaded to bring you sorrow. Moses was here last night after you were asleep. He told your father that God is sending another plague—the last one. It is coming tonight. And then we are to go."

Miriam turned away impatiently. "Oh, those horrid plagues!" she said angrily. "Zelda's father doesn't believe that Moses has anything to do with them, nor our God either. He says they just happen! But anyhow, Mother, those plagues don't come to Goshen. Our cattle didn't die, and our men were not sick. When the dreadful hailstorm came that spoiled all the gardens of Egypt it didn't touch us. Zelda's father says we just happened to be out of its path. And don't you remember when that awful darkness came, it was all light in Goshen?"

"But you, my child, are wanting to go out of Goshen tonight of all nights! Listen, my child, though it breaks your heart, I must tell you. This plague is different from all others. Our God is passing through Egypt tonight to take the eldest son in every house. Only where he sees the sign of blood on the door will he pass over."

Miriam stood with suddenly blanched face, her hands clasped at her throat, a great fear growing in her eyes. "Oh, Mother! Not *every* house. He wouldn't take Balthazar, would he?"

"He said every house," answered the mother sadly. "From the house of Pharaoh upon the throne, to the house of the maid behind the mill. Those were his very words."

"Oh, Mother, not Balthazar! Don't say he will take Balthazar! Why I was to dance with him tonight! And he is sending me flowers!"

Suddenly down the path came flying footsteps. A

tap sounded upon the door, and Zelda, bright-faced and eager, burst into the room.

"Why don't you come, Miriam? You promised to be over long before this, and where is Joseph? Balthazar says the sun is high and the flowers will droop if they are not picked right away. Won't you call Joseph, and you both come at once?"

"I—can't come, Zelda," murmured Miriam, white-lipped, lifting eyes brimming with tears.

"You can't come? Why? What is the matter? You promised! I am depending on you."

"Zelda—something has happened! We have—a feast—tonight. I did not know about it before. And —we are going on a journey. But—oh—Zelda! It is something more than that! *Another plague is coming tonight.*"

"Another plague! How silly. I thought I had you all over that nonsense. How could you know a plague was coming, and why should that make any difference anyway? Are you a coward? We can take care of you if anything happens, though I don't believe it will."

"You don't understand, Zelda. This plague is different. Our God will pass through Egypt, and take the oldest son from every house unless the sign is over the door."

"How ridiculous!" laughed Zelda, with a sneer upon her lovely face. "My brother is well and strong. What do you think could happen to him between now and tomorrow morning? I told you all your family were superstitious, and now I know it. There! There is Joseph now in the yard with your father! I'm going out to make him come home with me. He has common sense. He won't be afraid to come."

She turned toward the door, her gaze still out the window, but suddenly stopped and drew back, her hands pressing at her throat.

"Oh," she cried out in fright, "what are they doing to that darling little white lamb? Isn't that the lamb your father had penned up, the one without a single spot? They're not going to *kill* it, are they? Oh, why does your mother let them do that? That poor little lamb! I think they are cruel! Oh, see! There is blood!" She pressed her fingers against her closed eyes. "I cannot bear the sight of blood! It makes me feel faint!"

Then, opening her eyes almost against her will, she looked again. "Why are they dipping that bunch of hyssop in the lamb's blood? Why are they doing that? Miriam, do you see? They are smearing it all over the doorposts and over the lintel. Why doesn't your mother go out and stop them? What an awful thing to do! *Blood!*"

"It is our God's command," said Miriam solemnly. " 'When I see the blood, I will pass over you,' he said. It is to save my brother's life, Zelda."

Zelda looked at her scornfully. "How could blood on a doorpost possibly save anybody?" she asked.

"You tell her, Mother," said Miriam, suddenly dropping into a chair, her head buried in her arms on the window sill, her shoulders shaking with sobs.

"Zelda, dear, it isn't that blood out there that saves Joseph's life. That blood is only a sign of our faith in a promise made long ago. Our God promised that some day he would send One who would be a lamb slain for the sins of the world, and that through his death all who believed would be saved. And so, when we put this blood on the door at his command tonight it is a sign that we trust in the blood of the Lamb that is to come. We are putting ourselves under the blood covenant, where we know we are safe. Do you understand?"

Then Miriam rose earnestly, with clasped hands and pleading eyes looking into the angry, startled face of her friend. "Oh, Zelda, won't you go home right away and ask your father to kill a lamb and put the blood on your door? For perhaps God will see it and will pass over your house too, and your brother will be saved! Oh, won't you, Zelda?"

But Zelda met her with hard indignant eyes a-blaze. "What! Put blood on our doorposts when I am going to have a dance? Why the guests would soil their beautiful garments! Now I know that you are not only superstitious but crazy! I hate you! I never want to see you anymore," and she dashed out of the door and down the path toward her home.

All day long as Miriam went about her work with tears raining down her white cheeks, her heart was aching with sorrow. As she prepared the bitter herbs for the feast, and made the unleavened bread, her eyes kept turning toward the lattice that looked over to Egypt hoping against hope that perhaps, after all, Zelda had told her father. Perhaps before it was too late he might bring a lamb and put the needed sign upon his door also.

But the day went steadily on and she did not see

him. The afternoon was on the wane. The house was full of the smell of roasting lamb. The clothing was stacked in convenient bundles for sudden going. Father and brother brought the sheep and cattle from the fields, and neighbors hurried by doing the same, their faces filled with grave apprehension.

Miriam, as she laid the table for the passover feast, kept looking out the window toward the house across the way. She saw the caterers arrive, and a little later the orchestra carrying their instruments. She choked back her tears and wished that she dared pray to the God whom she had neglected.

Lights were springing up in the big house. Guests in bright garments were arriving. Once she was sure she saw Balthazar standing in the open door, silhouetted against a blaze of light, directing the servant of a guest about his camel. Her heart leaped up with great longing to go and beg Balthazar to do something before it was too late! But it was too late now, with guests arriving over there for the dance, and the feast about to be served in her own home. Too late!

The passover feast was ready. The roasted lamb, with the bitter herbs and unleavened bread, was set upon the table. The relatives had arrived who were to eat the lamb with them. They were all gathered about the solemn meal, and Miriam's father lifted his hands to ask a blessing on the feast. Into the hush of that moment broke the music of the orchestra in the Egyptian house, and when Miriam lifted her eyes she could see the bright lights and the moving figures as the dancing began.

The night went on. The solemn feast came to a close. The midnight hour drew near and Israel waited with a hush of awe upon her homes.

Miriam, suddenly glancing up at her brother Joseph, saw a look of wonder and exaltation upon his face such as she had never seen before. He was like one who has been set apart from others by some great act. There was a solemn beauty in his face that filled her with amazement.

Then her heart suddenly stood still. For the orchestra across the way crashed into utter silence, and into the foreboding hush caused by its ceasing there came frightened voices, frantic calls, and she could see hurrying forms running hither and thither. A light sprang up on the housetop where she knew Balthazar had his room.

Then, into the listening night, there rose a cry of anguish such as never had been heard before, reaching from the house across the hedge to the next house, and the next house, and the next, all across the borders of Goshen. Egypt weeping for her sons whom the death angel had taken.

As they listened, with white faces lifted in awe and fear, there came a sound of footsteps flying down the path. The door burst open without ceremony, and Zelda burst in, her arms laden with bright silken garments, and her hands filled with chains and bracelets and jewels.

She rushed up to Miriam. "Here! Take these, Miriam," she cried with anguish in her eyes. "Take them quick, and ask your father to get the people to go quickly! Oh, Miriam! My brother—is—*dead!*"

Then she turned and fled back to her desolated home.

Solemnly the procession moved along. Out into the night went Miriam. Out under the far cold stars. Out toward the Red Sea and the wilderness, and a grave in the wilderness. Out following that pillar of fire!

Miriam in her place in the march was glad of the darkness to hide her tears. For every step of the way this one wish beat itself into her soul: "Oh, if I had only told them about our God before it was too late! If only I had *lived* the faith which my fathers believed! Ah, if I had *had* a faith of my own to live; I might have led them to believe also! But how could I teach them when instead I was walking in their ways?"

And then, suddenly, Miriam understood why God had commanded his people to be a separated people, his peculiar people, a royal generation, not expected to find their joy in the things of the world about them. It was because they had been called to higher, better things, promised by him whose word could not be broken—and the promise was sealed with blood!

THE WEDDING GARMENT

MARTHA WORTH came out of her house one afternoon in early spring, hesitated a moment on the doorstep, looking up and down the street for a taxi, and then decided to walk. At the last minute her car had developed engine trouble. If she waited for repairs she would be late to her various appointments. She hated to be late. She prided herself that she had so systematized everything about her that her life moved as on oiled wheels.

She was meticulously dressed. Every item of her costume was carefully considered and in perfect harmony with every other detail. Martha was always ready with her garments for each changing season as it came.

Her dress was just the right shade of brown cloth trimmed with flat cream-colored fur, altogether the most correct thing for that season. The chic little hat of imported brown straw with its two creamy gardenias under the tilted lacy brim was most becoming, and exactly matched the smart little brown shoes, as the soft doeskin gloves exactly matched the fur jabot about her neck.

If she had any makeup on her face it was so skillfully applied that even a connoisseur was left in doubt as to whether it was not just natural perfection.

Martha stepped gracefully down the street, fully conscious of her own charming appearance, and more than one woman from car or bus or sidewalk, or even hidden behind a sheltering window drapery along the way, watched her with envious eyes, and longed to be like her.

Inside her dainty purse was a gold mounted tablet on which were written her engagements for the afternoon. She was to read a paper at a missionary meeting at half past two. It contained a careful study of the topography of Mohammedan lands, intricate and accurate statistics of the cost of maintaining missions, and the comparative number of natives Christianized. She had figured to a fraction just how much it cost to Christianize each one. The paper would take twenty minutes to read and she had carefully arranged to have it placed first on the program after the opening exercises so that she might slip out and meet her other engagements. She was due at a committee meeting of a charitable organization at three-thirty, and she hoped to be through with that by four. With good management she ought to be able to stop at the orphanage and perhaps drop in to Judge Warren's office to see that poor widow who ought to have a pension, before appearing at the

Verlenden-Braithwaite tea for a few minutes. All these engagements fitted well together and her costume was quite right for all. A trifle more than was necessary for the missionary meeting, perhaps—there would be only a few quiet, plain old ladies there, who would scarcely appreciate the cut of her imported ensemble, the real distinction of her whole outfit. Still, that was the beauty of costly simplicity. It did not look out of place anywhere.

As she walked down the pleasant street she was thinking of her plans for the coming week. How well she had arranged them. The dressmakers were coming just before the Barnwell wedding in plenty of time to finish her new lace dress. It was a little awkward having had to ask that Mrs. White on Sylvan Avenue to change time with her. But of course Mrs. White wouldn't be going to that wedding.

She turned into the main avenue now where there were plenty of taxis. But it was only five blocks farther, and she had plenty of time, so it was hardly worthwhile taking a taxi.

But even as she glanced at her wristwatch to make sure, a prankish breeze took liberties with her delicate hat, pulling her hair out from its precise arrangement about her lovely forehead, and tossing her jabot full in her face.

Martha looked up annoyed and discovered the sky suddenly overcast, and a drop of rain fell into her eye. April, of course. But how unexpected!

Another and another great drop splashed down. Her new ensemble! Would the cloth spot? She started to run, but the wind caught her on one side and the rain on the other and ran with her. All the taxis seemed suddenly to have fled from the avenue. She cast about for a quick shelter and backed into a convenient doorway.

There were others scurrying for this shelter also, many of them, and they crowded her inside the doors. She found herself in a church entrance with the big audience room just behind her, its doors standing wide and people crowding into the seats. There was a meeting going on, but it was not her church.

People were crowding her more and more. A man closed a dripping umbrella directly over her Paris hat and someone stepped harshly on the toe of her lovely new shoe.

"If you will step inside and take a seat you will not be in danger of getting so wet, Madam," said another man in a damp overcoat. Martha retreated into the far corner of a back seat.

Suddenly the audience burst forth into music, and the gladness of it was almost annoying.

Jesus may come today,
Glad day! Glad day!—

She shuddered involuntarily as she drew back into her corner under the gallery. What a startling, unpleasant thought to be flung into the orderliness of her spring day! It was unseemly, singing of the Lord in this familiar way. What a cataclysmic thing it would be to have Christ return to earth in the midst of the everyday work and program. How upsetting! She put the idea away with distaste.

The man who prayed seemed almost too intimate with God. Who were these people? Some peculiar cult that had hired the church for a conference, perhaps?

They burst into song again, every word distinct and clear:

He is coming again! He is coming again!
This very same Jesus, rejected of men—

There it was again, another hymn on that same theme! Could it be just a happening? But no, they were reading the Scripture: "In a moment, in the twinkling of an eye, at the last trump—"

Was it possible that anybody really took those words literally? *Now? Today?* How incongruous!

What was this meeting into which she had stumbled? A fanatical convention? She looked about the audience room, crowded now to overflowing. There were many people whom she knew, people of wealth and culture, some from her own church. Why, there was Judge Warren up toward the front of the church! And there was Mary, her dear friend! Mary was a saint. Mary was not a fanatic. Could it be that Mary believed such queer things, or had she, too, come in just for shelter from the rain?

Her meditations were arrested by a strong, tender voice from the platform:

"We know that our Lord Jesus is coming back to earth in visible form, first because he said he would: 'Let not your heart be troubled. . . . If I go and prepare a place for you I will come again, and receive you unto myself.' "

Martha sat up startled and began to listen, an anxious little frown between her eyes. She had earned a New Testament at the age of five for learning this fourteenth chapter of John, but never had she dreamed it had any reference to a literal return of the Lord. Outside the rain was pouring down, but she did not hear it. She was listening to this strange new doctrine. In all the years of her placid churchgoing twice a Sunday, she had never heard this doctrine preached before! Was it something new? Did people generally believe it? Passages of Scripture, words and phrases that suggested a possible coming of some One in the dim and misty future ages—she had always looked upon them as figures of speech, a fantastic picture language.

"The angels testified that Jesus would come again," said the speaker. " 'This same Jesus which is taken from you, up into heaven, shall so come in like manner as ye have seen him go into heaven.'

"And Paul gave his testimony later: 'In a moment, in the twinkling of an eye, at the last trump: for the trumpet shall sound, and the dead shall be raised incorruptible, and we shall be changed.' "

Martha shuddered, but the clear voice went steadily on repeating strangely familiar words that had never meant a thing to her before.

" 'For the Lord himself shall descend from heaven with a shout, with the voice of the archangel, and with the trump of God: and the dead in Christ shall rise first: then we which are alive and remain shall be caught up together with them in the clouds, to meet the Lord in the air; and so shall we ever be with the Lord. Wherefore comfort one another with these words.' "

Martha caught nothing of the comfort that these words were meant to be. She heard only the announcement of what to her seemed a catastrophe for which she was unprepared. She sat up sharply and listened with a startled pink spot glowing on each cheek as the verses multiplied. The man was actually stating that one out of every twenty-five verses in the New Testament referred to the return of the Lord. Surely that could not be so or she would have heard other ministers preaching about it. Could this one be right and all the others wrong?

The speaker went on to unfold prophecy. Martha had never heard before that the fig tree in the Bible always typified the Jewish people as a nation. She listened in amazement as the speaker reminded his audience that Jesus, when questioned of the times and seasons, had told his disciples that when they should see the fig tree putting forth leaves they were to know that his coming was close at hand. Surely this was farfetched, she thought, to take this symbolic language literally and think that it had any reference to the present-day effort of the Jews to establish a national home in Palestine. The speaker even dared to state that one of the main reasons for the world war was that Palestine might be once more in hands friendly to the Jews. He reminded his hearers that as soon as this was accomplished the war stopped.

Martha cast a hasty indignant glance about to see how the rest of the audience received this startling statement about the great world war in which men died to make the world safe for democracy. Think of all those bronze tablets everywhere, and the marble triumphal arches bearing the names of heroes, all the knitting, and the Red Cross bandages, and going without sugar in coffee, just to give Palestine back to the Jews! Ridiculous! An impertinence! Surely someone would get up and protest at this. But everyone was listening in eager absorption. Even her friend Mary wore a look of rapt exaltation.

And now Martha's attention was caught again. In quick succession, like spirits out of the past, came other proofs of the near approach of the great event, history written hundreds of years in advance, that was being fulfilled to the very letter. The records of fulfillment, many of them, were gathered out of the daily papers, events of which she herself had read. She had already recognized the worldwide tendency toward confederation under one head, found among nations, corporations, and organizations of every kind. She had, in fact, written a paper recently on that very subject and read it before the current events section of the women's club, for Martha Worth was a well-read, thinking woman, known to be up to date on politics and international affairs. But this astounding speaker dared to affirm that this tendency must surely lead in time to the coming of a great superman, a world ruler, who should be none other than the Antichrist of the Bible.

Martha had to admit, as she listened to verses of Scripture, that the League of Nations had certainly been prophesied. She heard with increasing horror the words concerning the "Prince of Rosh," the ruling spirit of Russia, who would spread terror from the north. She suddenly realized the tremendous significance of the revived importance of Rome. She heard for the first time about the two seasons of rainfall in Palestine, the "former" or early rain, and the "latter" rain late in the year which had ceased long ago "according to the word of the Lord," causing desolation in the land. She heard the prophecy read that it would surely not return until the Lord's approach was near; heard how it had most amazingly returned within recent years, only a few drops the first year, a little more the second, until now it had attained its normal fall, making a great change in the fertility of the land, "according to the word of the Lord."

With bated breath, sitting far forward in her seat, utterly unmindful of the rain outside, or of her unfulfilled engagements, she listened to those astonishing words of Paul to Timothy:

"This know also, that in the last days perilous times shall come. For men shall be lovers of their own selves, covetous, boasters, proud, blasphemers, disobedient to parents, unthankful, unholy, without natural affection, trucebreakers, false accusers, incontinent, fierce, despisers of those that are good, traitors, heady, high-minded, lovers of pleasures more than lovers of God; having a form of godliness, but denying the power thereof."

Instance after instance of the fulfillment of these things occurred to Martha as she listened with troubled, unbelieving eyes fixed upon the speaker, while he made clear how these words fit the present time.

And then, education! Increase of knowledge! Mechanical inventions! Airplanes, automobiles! Why, it was extraordinary that the Bible prophecies had held promise of all this throughout the ages and nobody had ever noticed it before!

And lastly she heard about the apostasy of the church. That phrase never had meant a thing to her before. Indeed she doubted if she had ever heard it. Now it seemed blasphemy! She could not believe that the Bible had really said that about the church, the holy church, that it should become apostate! Why, if the church was all wrong, what was left? Surely the church was doing more than ever today! She had heard many preachers tell how it was making the world better and better.

But this speaker struck at many of the activities and organizations of the day that she considered as sacred as the Bible and the church itself. She grew indignant. There were the activities that made up her whole life! They were the things upon which she relied to make sure her heavenly calling!

Rapidly the thrilling address drew to a close with wonderful, frightening words of how Christ was coming first to the air to take away the true church, the church that was not apostate. That implied that not all church members, not even all active church members, would belong to the church invisible, the body of Christ, which eventually would be caught up to meet the Lord in the air.

Indignation and fear struggled in her heart as she listened to the description of what would follow the sound of that silver trumpet. The dead arising! Her eyes filled with sudden tears. A kind of horror seized her at the thought of being caught up that way with the dead! But they would be *alive*—and of course she would not want to be left out if such a thing were really going to be, if it really had the sanction of well thinking, right living people of God! Of course she would be one of those who belonged to the Lord. She had always been an active Christian worker. Why, she had always been present to teach her Sunday school class, even when she had been out at a party till two or three o'clock Sunday morning. Even when she had no time to study her lesson she had always asked the questions in the lesson leaf faithfully and told her girls to look them up for next Sunday when they couldn't answer them. Of course, she didn't always remember to ask if they had, but—well she had always been faithful to her Sunday school class.

With the last word of warning, "Watch!" ringing in her ears, she rose with the rest for the closing hymn:

It may be at morn, when the day is awaking,
When sunlight through darkness and shadow is breaking,
That Jesus will come in the fullness of glory,
To receive from the world "His own."
O Lord Jesus, how long, how long, ere we shout the glad song,
Christ returneth! Hallelujah! hallelujah! Amen.

Then, with a frightened hunger in her soul, she turned reluctantly to go back to her world.

She was halfway home before she remembered her appointments for the afternoon. The missionary meeting! It would have been over long ago! She looked at her watch, *half past four!* She could scarcely believe her eyes. She held the watch to her ear to make sure it was still going. Half past four! She had been in that odd meeting over two hours. The charitable association would have adjourned at four, and the orphanage visitors' hours would be over too before she could get there. Judge Warren had been in the meeting, so he would not be in his office and she could not go there. There was nothing of her afternoon's program left but the tea, and somehow she felt strangely out of harmony with the atmosphere of a tea. She had a longing to rush home to her Bible and try to look up some of those references the speaker had quoted, just to prove they were not there.

Of course it was all a hoax. Some kind of new doctrine that would soon be shown up as dangerous and disturbing. She wished she had written down the references, but they would surely be easy to find; they were so odd they would shout at one from the pages. She had a vague notion that one of them was in Job and another in Revelation, and weren't some of them in those little books at the end of the Old Testament that one could never find? But she had a concordance somewhere in her library. She would find them.

When she reached home she went to work at once,

not even waiting to take off her new hat and coat. She turned the leaves of her Bible rapidly. Revelation caught her eye, and suddenly she halted at a verse. Ah! Here was one they had missed at the meeting, but somehow it had a sinister tone. How had they missed this? "Behold I come as a thief. Blessed is he that watcheth, and keepeth his garments, lest he walk naked, and they see his shame."

A chill went through her. Garments! Would one have to prepare garments for such a time?

Martha had no knowledge of dispensational truth. She was not aware that Christ does not come to his own as a thief, but as a heavenly Bridegroom. She saw only that awful word, "I come," reiterated, and a foreboding filled her.

Turning the leaves rapidly again to the end of the book, she came on another verse: "He which testifieth these things saith: Surely, I come quickly! Amen." And then that lilt of an answer—so strange that anyone could feel that way! "Even so, come, Lord Jesus." But of course, that was for those who were watching, probably, and had their garments all ready. But she shuddered. That picture of walking naked before the assembled world at such a time was terrible! She must get rid of all these notions immediately. She would go and find Mary and talk it over with her. Mary was sane, and Mary was a saint. Mary would dispel this gloom. She must get into a better frame of mind before Tom came home.

So she put away her Bible and went to Mary's house.

Mary had just come home from the meeting and

was sitting with her Bible and notebook going over the references.

Mary greeted her joyously.

"Oh, you were out this afternoon, weren't you? Wasn't it wonderful! I tried to reach you after it was over, but somebody held me up, and when I reached the door you were gone."

"Wonderful?" echoed Martha in amazement. "Who is he? What is he? Mary, do you believe all that? Do really nice people believe it?"

"Believe it? You mean believe that Christ is coming soon? Why, of course. It is the blessed hope of Christians, dear. Don't you believe it? It is one of the articles of the faith of our church, you know. Most Christians throughout the ages have believed it, haven't they?"

"I'm sure I don't know," said Martha crossly. "I never heard of it before. That is, I never supposed for an instant that anyone took those verses seriously. I never heard a minister preach on it, and I've been going to church regularly since I was a child."

"I know," said Mary sadly. "It does seem as if many ministers are afraid of it. I wonder why? But lately, dear, I've been hearing it a lot. There have been several other speakers on the subject in the city the last month or two. One from Australia, this one from London, and two men from our own land."

"But do you really mean that you believe all that man said? You think Christ is literally coming to earth—and *soon?*"

"I certainly do!" said Mary with a solemn gladness in her voice and a light in her eyes. "Isn't it glorious!"

Martha studied her friend's face with troubled eyes.

"Well, then," she asked at last with an anxious sigh, "if that is really so, how would one go about getting ready? What would one—*wear* on such an occasion?"

"Oh," laughed Mary happily. "We don't have to worry about that. That's all taken care of. If we are his own, and included in that wonderful meeting in the air, our garments are all provided for us."

Martha stiffened with dignity.

"What do you mean, provided for us? I couldn't think of accepting a costume for that or any other occasion. No self-respecting person would. It would be like renting a wedding suit. I always believe in preparing for all occasions. A well-ordered person will be prepared for every emergency. My mother always kept a shroud in the house in case of sudden death in the family. But can't you tell me what would be expected? Isn't there something said about it in the Bible? I thought it was very odd that he didn't tell us how to be prepared."

" 'That I may be found *in him,'* " quoted Mary softly.

"Oh, yes, of course," said Martha sharply, "but I mean, *really*. Don't you know what we are supposed to wear? What is the material?"

"Oh, yes," said Mary quietly, "white linen, of course."

"Linen!" Martha looked annoyed. "You don't really mean linen—*handkerchief* linen, perhaps? But wouldn't that wrinkle awfully?"

"It's *righteousness,* you know," explained Mary gravely.

Martha caught at the word.

"Oh, I see," said she with relief. "Well, that's not so hard. Thank you so much. But I must be getting home. If this thing is really coming off soon, I'll have to get to work."

"But, dear," said Mary anxiously, "you don't understand. You don't have to provide a garment. Christ has provided it himself. He says—"

"But I tell you I couldn't think of accepting that. It may be well enough for some poor, sick, ignorant, incapable souls, but I take it he expects more of those who have been better taught. Doesn't it say something about working out your own salvation? Good-bye, I must hurry. It is almost time for Tom to be home and I have to look over the dinner table to see if the spoons and forks are all on. We have a new maid and she is always making mistakes. Tom does get so upset when the table isn't set right."

Mary stood at the door and watched her friend go down the street, repeating thoughtfully, sorrowfully to herself the words:

"For I bear them record that they have a zeal of God, but not according to knowledge. For they, being ignorant of God's righteousness, and going about to establish their own righteousness, have not submitted themselves unto the righteousness of God. For Christ is the end of the law for righteousness unto every one that believeth."

Martha went home and sat down with her Bible

and concordance again, looking up righteousness. Ah, here was a verse:

"I put on righteousness and it clothed me. My judgment was as a robe and a diadem."

That was comforting. She had always been praised for her good judgment.

And here was another in Revelation:

"For the marriage of the Lamb is come, and his wife hath made herself ready, and to her was granted that she should be arrayed in fine linen, clean and white, for the fine linen is the righteousness of the saints."

So, Mary was right, linen was a symbol of righteousness. And she, Martha, was probably accounted a saint, in the heavenly accounting. Saint Martha! That sounded good.

Martha sat for some minutes looking off into space, thinking over her own virtues, and the many good deeds that were against her name, until her husband came and she arose with a sigh of satisfaction, her gloom all dispelled.

Tom had brought a man home to dinner with him and they had a fine evening together. Martha forgot all about the happenings of the afternoon and her disturbed thoughts. Not until they had retired for the night and the lights were out did she remember anything about it. Suddenly she spoke out in the darkness:

"Tom, did you know there were people who believe that Christ is coming back to earth again?"

"Poppycock!" said Thomas sleepily.

"No, but really, Tom. Our church believes it. It's a part of the faith."

"Well, they've kept mighty good and still about it if they do," laughed Thomas. "Where have you been this afternoon? We'll have you putting on a white nightgown and sitting on a fence rail to watch for an opening in the sky pretty soon if you get started on such notions. Don't you know there were a lot of nuts who had that in their heads several years ago and went to the dogs over it? Sold all they had and nearly starved to death! Went crazy when it didn't happen the way they had planned! For heaven's sake, cut it out! I want to get some sleep!"

Martha said no more, but she couldn't stop thinking, so she began to consider all that she had done to make the world better. Surely she would not lack for material for the right garments. At last she dropped into an uneasy sleep.

Sometime in the night she thought she heard a distant sound, clear, sweet, *peremptory* like a trumpet! She sat up instantly in bed with the thought, "Can that be the trump of God?" It came again, more clearly, and she thought, "He is come and I am not ready!" What could she do quickly in this emergency? It was the first time in her life that she had been caught unprepared for any great event.

Then she thought she remembered two chests in the attic, carefully put away from dust and moth. One was labeled VIRTUES and the other GOOD DEEDS. She must get to them quickly and somehow array herself before it was too late, so she should not walk naked and be ashamed.

She thought she took her bedroom candle and crept softly toward the stairs. She must not waken Tom yet, not till she was sure. She dreaded his sarcasm. If this should turn out not to be the trump of God she would never hear the last of it!

In the dim, dusty attic she set down her candle on an old trunk, and opened the chests. First the one labeled VIRTUES. Yes, right there on the very top lay the diadem of her judgment, catching rays from the candlelight and flinging them back into her sleep-filled eyes. That would be lovely for a coronet. And there was her sweet temper lying next, a placid necklace of pearls. And her perseverance! That had brought her much praise from the church officers, though her husband would insist on calling it persistence. But it would stand her in good stead now, a soft, firm garment. Ah, she had accomplished many things for good purposes through that virtue. Next was a bright little gold girdle of truth, and anklets of churchgoing on Sunday, bracelets of kindness, feathers of smiles and pleasant words—oh, there was plenty of material here for adornment.

She turned to the other chest and took out her good deeds. There was a shining piece of golden silk that stood for adherence to the commandments, laced with a ribbon of blue and with fringe on the border. Oh, she had kept the letter of the law most scrupulously. And there was a piece of white linen. She seized upon it eagerly. That must be for the outer robe. Its border was made of cunning needlework representing the many things that she had done for church and state. A little intricate design of flowers and faces, and scenes from her life. There, for instance, was her Sunday school class, bright, happy young girls, and the boys who belonged in their crowd. How often she had gathered them for good times, always insisting that it should be in the name of the church, with allegiance to its outward forms. They danced along the border of that linen fabric in bright silk colors, their very expressions portrayed in detail. And then the procession merged into a scene more grave. These were the men who had come to her for work when times were hard, the ones she had fed and helped, the wives and mothers for whom she had found shelter and food and labor, the orphanage for whom she had begged dolls and toys, the members of her charitable organization who had done her homage, the people she had called upon in the every-member canvass; and mingled with them all the flowers she had provided for the church, for the sick, and the sad—a garland for the border.

Hark! Was that a nearer trumpet sound? With trembling hands she slipped the garments over her head, threw them quickly about her shoulders, and draped around her waist and shoulders the lengths of embroidered white linen, donned necklaces, bracelets, the diadem upon her forehead, slipped her feet into a pair of golden shoes wrought delicately of the adulation of her own small world, and stood ready, listening.

Another peal of silver sound came trembling nearer, and she snatched up an armful of white linen from the chest. Tom would need something at the last minute, and of course would look to her to provide it—blame her, perhaps, if it were not close at hand.

She stooped to pick up her candle and hurry down the stairs, for the silver sound was coming close now and filled all the dusty attic shadows with a thrilling wonder.

But suddenly a blinding light shone round about her, a light so great that it fairly overwhelmed her. She closed her eyes and could not look at first, but gradually she grew accustomed to the brightness, and knew that it was glory, God's glory. What was it doing here in her attic? Ah, God had seen that she was ready, dressed in her own righteousness. Saint Martha! Her heart swelled with pride! She lifted her head with new courage and looked at the glory. Lo, it was a mirror and herself reflected in it!

With pride she looked with open face to see herself. But—what was this? A poor, frightened, ghastly face, a gaunt figure draped in tattered, soiled garments, dirty, besmirched, disgusting!

She put a trembling hand down and felt for her linen robe, ran a quivering finger over the embroidered border, watching herself in the glass to make sure it was herself she saw. Where were the golden threads that had been woven so cunningly among the flowers? Tarnished! Blackened! Spoiled! And the flowers were faded, their glorious colors sickly in the glory light! The linen itself was dirty and dropping in tatters! The brightness of his glory in the room showed all the destruction that she had not seen in the fond satisfaction of her own little candlelight.

She looked at her own image more closely now, with failing heart, and saw her very face and hands were thick with soil, the dust of the attic upon her brow, and in sudden humiliation and fear she dropped upon her knees.

Then a Voice spoke, out of the silence and glory:

"All our righteousnesses are as filthy rags!"

The words went through her soul like a sword. She looked again toward the One who seemed to stand there before her, with his glory like a mirror, and saw the sin stains upon herself, saw that the filthy rags were unfit covering in which to appear before the Lord of Glory.

Then a strange thing happened. In the silence of that glory-filled attic, Martha knelt and began to understand that all things for which she had striven, all her former ideals, wishes, ambitions, pride, even her good works and virtues were worth nothing. There was only one thing worthwhile in the whole world, and that was to know Christ.

Suddenly, out of the memory of her childhood came words that spoke themselves to her very soul again with a new meaning that thrilled her as she had never been thrilled before:

"But what things were gain to me, those I counted loss for Christ. Yea, doubtless, and I count all things but loss . . . that I may win Christ, and be found *in* him, not having mine own righteousness, which is of the law, but that which is through the faith of Christ, the righteousness which is of God by faith."

Then all at once the room was filled once more

with the soft silver sound of trumpets, and golden angelic voices began to sing:

When He shall come with trumpet sound,
Oh, may I then in Him be found!
Dressed in His righteousness alone,
Faultless to stand before His throne.
  On Christ the solid rock I stand,
  All other ground is sinking sand.

THE DIVIDED BATTLE

THE forces of darkness had been quietly working in Morningtown for months. At last they were drawn up in the open with shining armor, glancing sabers. Appalling hosts—file after file in battle array! Something had to be done about it, and done quickly, or Morningtown would disappear, its Christian citizens would fall before the onslaught of the enemy, and the witness which had been established in their score or more of evangelical churches would be wiped out.

On the ramparts of heaven, bright angels were watching, numbering the hosts of darkness, turning eager eyes toward the Christian people of Morningtown to see how their faith would stand in this great testing, waiting for orders from the Throne. Here and there an angel could be seen through the golden mist of the heights, winging his way downward on an errand of vital importance to Morningtown.

Overnight Morningtown had come to the knowledge of the invasion. Dark sleuths had been seen for sometime, it is true, skulking about the streets, talking with some of the weaker of the saints, winning one here and there; but the right-minded people of the town had not taken the danger seriously until the army was actually upon them.

The Reds, the peril from Russia? Oh, yes, the Bible mentioned that in a vague way, and overzealous Bible students had occasionally made a brief ripple in the monotony of placid Christian minds by suggesting that the prophecy concerning the Prince of Rosh who should come down from the north and spread peril might be actually upon them; but for the most part the Christians had smiled and gone their way. It might be that sometime something like peril could come from such things, but it wasn't in the least likely that disaster in such crude form could come today in a civilized world. The nations would of course rise and prevent it. Some even asserted that all this talk about Communism was bosh. What was the matter with Communism? There were good things about Communism, weren't there? Of course, new things were always denounced for a while till people got used to them. Even Russia wasn't so bad.

"They say the people of Russia are very happy, and have things so beautifully regulated for them," said one sweet Morningtown matron, whose life was one long idle hour in which she did exactly what she pleased.

The gangsters? Oh, yes, of course, but gangsters didn't show themselves much in Morningtown, at least not until last week when a Morningtown lawyer had been abducted on his way to his office and a hundred-thousand-dollar ransom demanded. But that would soon be cleared up.

"Kidnapping ought to be punishable with death!" asserted a dapper businessman who hadn't been able to believe at first that the man had really been kidnapped.

"Why, certainly!" answered his wife and two women who were calling upon her. "But to think those wicked men would *dare* do a thing like that in *Morningtown!*"

Politics were beginning to seethe, even in Morningtown. The wrong man had been elected in a recent campaign, and was driving wedges here and there in the security that had heretofore hedged Morningtown. Licenses granted for horrors unheard of before in the quiet town had suddenly awakened smug, satisfied citizens. People were beginning to say that *something* ought to be done about it.

New cults had stolen in unaware, so subtly that people thought they were merely bright new forms of trite old worship; yet now they began to make inroads into the ranks of the orthodox faith. And when the state of things began to affect the finances of the churches, *then* the churches sat up and took notice. *Then* the ministers of the churches met together to consider what to do to combat the forces of evil that had come in.

It was early fall and the ministers had just gotten home from their vacations. They were feeling rested —some of them—and fit and ready for work. Most of them considered that it would be an easy matter to rout the enemy. So, at the call of one or two who were not so complacent about it, they had come together to consider what was to be done for the common protection and good of the community.

The meeting was held in the largest and richest church of Morningtown. It was called early, at nine o'clock, with a practical program in the morning, consisting of reports from the different districts of the city as to the devastation wrought in each quarter during the summertime.

The women of the Old First Church were busy in the basement preparing a luxurious luncheon for the noon hour adjournment. The afternoon program in the early hours was to consist of suggestions from various representative groups. Later they would consider some set plan of action prepared by a committee who had called the meeting. The committee was chaired by one, Curtius Goodwin, a man beloved by many. The evening was to be devoted to a great mass meeting to arouse the community to the need for fighting, and to announce plans.

Meantime the enemy were encamped over against Morningtown ready for battle. An attack was imminent and the angels were assembled on heaven's ramparts to watch the struggle and join in the triumph song.

Down in the basement kitchen of the church, Mrs. Green, Mrs. Bartholomew, Mrs. Jansen, and Mrs. Ridgeway were cutting up chicken and peeling potatoes.

"It's good we didn't try to have chicken salad today," said Mrs. Ridgeway, plopping a couple of drumsticks into the big kettle that stood before her on the table. "Men do hate cold dishes on a cold day, and see how really chilly it has turned since the storm last night."

"But chicken salad is a lot easier to serve," said wiry little Mrs. Jansen. "You don't have to bother keeping gravy hot. Oh, you're making soda biscuits, aren't you, Mrs. Green! That's nice! I always say stewed chicken isn't worth eating without lots of soda biscuits and gravy."

"We're having a regular spread today, aren't we?" said Mrs. Bartholomew. "I wonder why? What is it all about, anyway? I just got home last night and found a note my daughter-in-law had left for me saying they wanted me down at the church early this morning. What kind of a meeting are they having upstairs, anyway?"

"Oh, I don't know, really. Something about an evangelistic campaign, isn't it?" said Mrs. Ridgeway. "I suppose that Mr. Tupper of the Fifth Church is putting it on, and trying to get the rest of the churches to finance it. He is so officious, isn't he? I suppose he is a good man, but he has such a long lugubrious nose, and he is always wanting special prayer services and things. They say he is very spiritual, but somehow I never liked him. When he prays he always gets to crying and the tears drip off his nose. He doesn't wear awfully clean collars either."

"Now, Mrs. Ridgeway, how do you know the tears

drip off his nose if you are praying as you ought to be?" laughed Mrs. Green, mixing her baking powder and flour carefully.

They all laughed playfully.

"Oh, well, I don't see any great virtue in just keeping your eyes shut if you don't feel prayerful," said Mrs. Ridgeway amusedly, "and I never do when that man is praying, he sounds so sanctimonious."

"They say he gets a terribly small salary," put in Mrs. Jansen thoughtfully. "I suppose maybe he can't afford to have a washerwoman very often. He has a sick wife."

"Well, poor ministers shouldn't marry sick wives!" said Mrs. Ridgeway firmly. "And anyway, a man like that has no business in the ministry! Of course *he* wouldn't get an adequate salary, a man like that, with tears dripping off a long nose! I wonder the other ministers let him dictate, calling meetings together for somebody else to finance! I wonder they put up with it."

"But I heard it was Curtius Goodwin who called this meeting, not Mr. Tupper at all," said Mrs. Green.

"Well, it's the same thing. He's an elder in Tupper's church," said Mrs. Ridgeway. "You'll find Tupper's at the bottom of it! He always is of anything queer!"

"But they do say that Mr. Tupper is very spiritual!" said quiet little Mrs. Bowen who had just come in and was tying on a large gingham apron over her neat house dress, preparatory to shelling peas. "They say he is deeply taught in the Scriptures, too, and the people in his church love him dearly!"

"Oh, good morning, Mrs. Bowen!" said Mrs. Ridgeway, looking up from her chicken. "Are you on this committee, too? I thought you had your turn last spring."

"I did, but Mrs. Clark is sick and she asked me to take her place."

"Well, that's good. You're one of the best workers we've got, if I don't agree with you in your choice of spirituality. I've no objection to Mr. Tupper's spirituality if he stays in his place, but when he attempts to tell ministers like our Dr. Patton when it's time to have special services, I draw the line! Imagine a man like Mr. Tupper trying to manage men of the intellectual development of Dr. Patton! It's ridiculous! They're not in the same class."

"Say," said Mrs. Green lowering her voice a little and looking toward Mrs. Bowen, who was hanging up her hat and coat on a hook at the far end of the dining room, "I heard that people think our Dr. Patton is getting awfully modern. Had you heard that?"

"Well, if he is, I'm modern too!" snapped Mrs. Ridgeway, adding a handful of chicken wings to the pot. "I certainly think he's a better guide than that Mr. Tupper. But he isn't a modernist. I heard him say he wasn't! Probably the people who said he was didn't know a modernist from a stick of wood. I wonder if they are going to have an evangelist or just have the preachers take turns? It seems to me in these times of depression that they ought to consider expense. If they have an evangelist there'll be that continual harping on money, money, money! I for one haven't any money to give to anything extra! And I can't see why they need an evangelist or special meetings either."

"They do say the town is getting awful!" said Mrs. Green. "I guess they need it, all right, especially since liquor has come back."

"Nonsense! Pessimism. The town isn't any worse than it ever was, and it's all a lot of propaganda, I say! People like Mr. Tupper want to get into prominence, so they get up an idea that the town needs saving just so they can be great heroes and save it! They want to get their names connected with some big evangelist or great public speaker and have people ask them to pray and things, and get their pictures in the paper as being foremost in running the campaign! I know *one* at least who is always prominent in these things who generally gets the job of handling all the *money* that comes in. I guess you all know who I mean. I'm not mentioning any names." Mrs. Ridgeway slid the final piece of chicken into the pot and set it on the stove, carefully adjusting the gas flame to suit her need, amid a significant silence in the room. There were quick, furtive glances and lifted brows. Then she came back to wipe off the table for the next act.

"I wonder," she went on, "who they'll get if they have an evangelist. I'm sure I hope they won't try having that old Mr. Banning they had last summer. Of all the sob stuff! It was just the limit!"

"I heard they were thinking of asking Dr. Garthwaite. Wouldn't that be simply great? They say he's the most cultured speaker, and has the reputation of being the best Bible teacher this side of the water," offered Mrs. Spicer, who had just come in and was taking off her hat.

"Well, I guess that'll run into money," said Mrs. Jansen. "They say he never goes anywhere under a hundred dollars a night!"

"*A* hundred!" said Mrs. Ridgeway. "Better say *three* hundred, or even five sometimes! The idea of any man thinking he can preach even *a* hundred dollars' worth in one evening! In my opinion, any man who makes merchandise of the gospel isn't fit to preach! For my part, I'd like to have that Mr. McClain they had over at Craigstown last winter. He was interesting and good looking, and real snappy, and what's more, he knew when to stop! I hate these long, drawn out *appeals*. For my part, I would only be turned against religion if I were an unconverted person."

"I heard that Mr. McClain didn't get on well with his mother-in-law," offered Mrs. Green as she rubbed the shortening into her flour. "*I* think a man who can't get on with his own relatives hasn't any right to be preaching the gospel."

"Well, there *are* mothers-in-law!" laughed Mrs. Bartholomew, looking significantly toward Mrs. Spicer who had the reputation of nagging her daughter-in-law, though there wasn't a better worker, nor a more ardent member of the missionary society in the whole church.

"Well, Mr. McClain has a fine mother-in-law," said Mrs. Green eagerly. "My mother's cousin knows her well. She lives next door to her and she says she's perfectly *lovely*. She's the most saintly Christian she knows!"

"Do you mean that sickly looking Mrs. Faber?" snapped Mrs. Ridgeway. "My word! If you call *her* a Christian I'll give up! She has a tongue like a pair of manicure scissors. I'll own she can run a meeting, but there's plenty that can do that and haven't any more Christianity than my foot! For sweet pity's sake, don't judge an evangelist by the way he treats his mother-in-law!"

"Well," said Mrs. Green with an offended air, "I'm sure I don't care to go to the services if they have that man. I should be thinking of the way he treats that sweet little woman all the time. You can say what you like about her, but *I* happen to *know* her!"

"Yes, and so do *I!*" snapped Mrs. Ridgeway, slamming off to the dish closet and beginning to hand down piles of plates.

"Well, I wish they'd get that Mr. Brown from London. They say he's coming over this year and if we tried we could get him first of anybody. They say he's just *won*derful!" said Mrs. Jansen. "I'd like to hear somebody for once that had a big reputation like that!"

"Oh, but I heard he wasn't sound," lisped Mrs. Trevor, a pretty, golden-haired, glib-tongued young woman. "I heard he didn't believe in future punishment—I *think* that was it—or perhaps it was safety and security—or else he *didn't*, I'm not sure which it was, but I know they thought he wasn't sound. People in Morningtown would never agree to have him if he wasn't considered sound."

"Oh, but he *is!*" said Mrs. Green. "I heard the elders talking about him the other night. They say that's just something some enemies of his have got up about him."

"If there's any question there's *no* question!" said Mrs. Ridgeway severely, arriving back in the kitchen with her hands full of teaspoons. "What do you think, ladies, these teaspoons are all sticky! Can you imagine it? Who was on the committee last time? Mrs. Randall? I *thought* so. For my part I'd rather have less prayers and more cleanliness. The next time I hear her leading in prayer with that smug little holy smile and her eyes shut so sweetly, I'll think of those sticky teaspoons!"

There was a general laugh at this, and then Mrs. Green held up a warning finger to her lips.

"Sh!" she said under her breath. "There comes Mrs. Holmes. She's always scolding people for gossiping."

"Hm!" said Mrs. Ridgeway under her breath also. "She's not so holy as she looks! I heard her talking to the milkman this morning out the back door—she lives in the other half of my house—and my word! If that's Christianity, lead me from it!"

Mrs. Holmes advanced into the room smiling.

"Oh, there are a lot of you here already, aren't there? Well, I'm glad. You won't need me for a little while, will you? I do want to run upstairs to the gallery and listen to the devotional meeting. That minister from the new nondenominational church is going to lead it and they say he's perfectly *wonderful!* Why can't you all come? There's plenty of time. I'll come right down as soon as it's over and work hard. I was to set tables and there's plenty of time for that!"

"Thanks awfully!" said Mrs. Ridgeway curtly. "I prefer to stay here and do my duty. Besides, I'm not crazy about any fledglings just out of seminary—or Bible school. I guess he didn't even go to seminary, did he? They say he can't speak correct English. I heard he says 'lay' instead of 'lie'!"

"Oh, the idea! *Really?* I believe I'll run upstairs just a minute. I'd like to see what he's like!" said Mrs. Trevor, untying her frivolous pink and blue beribboned apron.

"*I* heard," said Mrs. Bartholomew when the significant smile that followed Mrs. Trevor's hasty exit had begun to fade, "I heard that the minister they have over at Exeter First is *divorced.* I wouldn't like to have a minister who was divorced, would you? It seems somehow unministerial, don't you think?"

"It seems unchristian!" snapped Mrs. Ridgeway. "I shouldn't care to listen to a man who upheld such standards. What would our country be coming to if the Christian religion closed its eyes to divorce? I wouldn't think a man like that ought to be allowed to sit in and vote with a body like what's meeting upstairs. I wonder if the other ministers know it?"

"Depends what they were divorced for!" said Mrs. Spicer slicing tart apples into the pie she was building.

"You don't even know he *is* divorced!" suggested Mrs. Jansen. "It might not be true. Anyhow, I think you ought to wait till you find out for sure before you condemn him."

"Where there's doubt there's usually *no* doubt," said Mrs. Ridgeway, primly shutting her thin lips. "Juliana Green, did you scald those kettles before you set the potatoes to cook in them? You can't trust the way the last committee washed up, remember."

Upstairs the devotional meeting was over and there was a little stir as the surreptitious attendants in the gallery stole out one at a time, through a swing door that needed oiling, and the ministers came to order to consider the program of the morning.

The ladies burst into the basement again with renewed vigor in their manner.

"That perfectly stunning new minister over at Third is there," said young Mrs. Trevor, fluttering into a chair and beginning to shell peas daintily. The peas were almost shelled and there was a possibility of an end sometime in view, so she chose to shell peas.

"He has the handsomest eyes!" she babbled on, "and they say his wife is darling! She's very active among the young people and shows them all sorts of good times at the manse. He preached at the open air meetings in the Park all summer and I just adored hearing him. They say his wife is very liberal."

"Yes," said Mrs. Green, "I guess she is. Mrs. Brown told me that she had a bridge party at the manse the other night. Three tables! Imagine that for a minister's wife! I'm glad she's not our minister's wife!"

"That's not so!" said Mrs. Holmes majestically, turning on her victim sternly. "I happen to know it's not so!"

"*How* do you know?" asked Mrs. Ridgeway.

"Because I *asked her,* if you want to know!" Mrs. Holmes' voice was calm. There was deep condemnation in the look she turned on Mrs. Ridgeway. "Mrs. Blynn who lives across the way from her came and told me that same tale you're telling. She said, just as you did, that there were *three* tables. She said she *saw* them playing. Three tables! And I said I *knew* it wasn't so. I happened to know that minister's reputation. I happened to know he and his wife are both opposed to worldly amusements, so I just went in and *asked* her."

"You went and *asked* her?" echoed Mrs. Trevor delightedly. "*What* did she say?"

"You went to the manse and *asked* her?" echoed several other ladies.

"I went to the manse and asked her!" responded Mrs. Holmes impressively. "And she just laughed. She sat down in a chair and laughed and *laughed,* and then she explained that her sister and her two cousins and their husbands had driven over from Ulster County and brought them a big new picture puzzle, and they were putting it together. She said they had used the little center table and the cutting table and the small table from the hall so there would be room enough for everybody to work at it, and they had the picture divided into three sections. It was a very large picture. She said they had a good deal of fun over it and sat up till they finished it, and that it took a long time. But she said she guessed she'd have to pull the curtains the next time she played with a picture puzzle."

There was a dead silence in the room for a moment, and then Mrs. Ridgeway with pursed lips said, "Well, I don't know but a Christian can waste as much time fiddling with a picture puzzle as playing bridge. I for one haven't any time for *either.* It's frivolous, especially in a minister! I really don't care to hear men preach who do foolish things like that!"

Said Mrs. Holmes with dignity, "It's high time the tables were set! Where are the tablecloths? Are you sure we have enough? There are a lot of men upstairs. I could run home and get a couple more tablecloths if you think we need them."

"You'd better stay here and *work,* if you ask me," said Mrs. Ridgeway grimly. "If there are more people up there than were *invited,* the rest of them can sit at bare tables, provided there's anything left for them to eat. Personally I have no time for these Christian scavengers, running anywhere they can get a meal for nothing!"

Then those women went swiftly to work setting the tables, and the pleasant clatter of dishes and pans covered their further conversation.

Out in the basement hallway, a couple of dark shadowy spies from the ranks of the enemy encamped about the town, stole silently, unseen, up the stairs, well satisfied with what they had already heard, one to listen further upstairs in the church, the other to hasten to his military head and report progress.

This was his report:

"So far all going well. The company hastily assembled from the ranks of Morningtown Christians to prepare for battle are already turning their swords against each other. Christian casualty list quite satisfactory. Many noted ministers, Bible teachers, and women of saintly reputation among the slain. People still blindly fighting each other, under the impression they are attacking the enemy."

The ministers came down to lunch well pleased with their own activity. They had heard the reports about the enemy in their midst with gravity, but they had little doubt that they would be able to cope with the adversary as soon as they were thoroughly organized. They all told a good many jokes and funny stories, and laughed immoderately as they devoured the chicken and biscuits to a wing, and added mashed potatoes and pickles and peas and tomato salad, and apple pie a la mode, washed down with cups and cups of coffee. All, that is, but a few of them who sat together conversing gravely with serious brows and earnest talk. They seemed almost sorrowful, and some of them scarcely bothered to eat, they were so absorbed and troubled.

The scout who returned to the enemy's headquarters at the close of the luncheon carried back a concise report of progress.

"Slaughter becoming general during noon hour. Many noted evangelists slain and their bodies thrown to the beasts of prey!"

During the afternoon session there were occasional surreptitious withdrawals from the audience, a minister here, an elder there, into the shadowy corners of the Sunday school room for quiet consultation. A careful watcher might have noticed that they were of the wealthier churches, and that the expressions they wore were not such as betokened peace and love. They talked by twos and threes in unnoticeable corners, and shook their heads meaningfully with sneering smiles. And when the plan of action drawn up and presented by Curtius Goodwin was read for approval, and came to a vote, these men mustered their forces for a protest.

One brother arose to plead for more time. He said there were many who would not agree that the evangelist selected was the wisest choice that could be made.

An elder went on to speak of two others on the list of speakers and cast slight aspersions on their spirituality and fitness for the honored task of leading Morningtown Christians on to the fight. At last all but a very few of the noble list of picked warriors lay wounded before the august company of Christians.

Discussion grew hot. Some very sharp words were exchanged. Some plain truths were told, and denied point blank, and a decision seemed no nearer than when the question was first proposed.

In the shadowy dimness back under the gallery two demon-emissaries of the enemy stood taking notes. One of them, young in his office, looked puzzled.

"I don't see how you tell which are Christians and

which are fighting for us," he said at last, in an aside to his superior officer, who was watching the argument with great satisfaction.

"Don't you know the rule?" asked the other sharply. "This is their own Leader's word: 'By this shall all men know that ye are my disciples, *if ye have love one to another*'!"

A look of surprised comprehension began slowly to dawn upon the young demon's face.

"Why, then almost all of these are fighting for us!" he said with a glance that took in the whole congregation.

"Yes, practically all of them, except a few that I seem to have lost sight of during the afternoon. I wonder if they have gone home? Come this way and let us look through the other rooms of the church. Not much account perhaps, but still it is my duty to watch them all."

They stole through the shadows and drifted here and there.

"I wonder what this door's shut for," said the young officer, pausing beside a closed door that opened into a classroom.

He listened a moment.

"Ha!" he said, and stole around into the adjoining room to peer through a crack where the partition had not been tightly closed.

"Put your eye to that crack!" he whispered. "I thought I'd find them up to something!"

The younger demon peered into the dark classroom and saw five men upon their knees praying. They did not appear to be great men; two of them were quite shabby, but they were praying mightily.

"What does that mean?" said the younger spirit, stepping back.

"It means," said the older one, "that they have a secret wire hidden somewhere over which they are sending messages back and forth to heaven. Didn't you hear them crying for reinforcements? And they'll get them, too—just those few plain men—because they keep in constant touch with their Leader. You don't find any of *them* wounding any of their own men. They have private information, and their eyes are constantly to God, their ears continually open for his guidance. We knew there was a leak somewhere and information was getting through our lines, but we couldn't exactly locate it. Now there are two other places I've got to watch and report about. Come on!"

He led the way down to the basement.

The luncheon was all cleared away and a supper was in process of evolution. The long tables were freshly reset. Platters of pink ham with parsley borders were at intervals along the tables, dishes of olives and celery, great plates of rolls, glass dishes of quivering jelly, lettuce-lined dishes of cole slaw, small dishes of squarely cut cheese. It was going to be a good supper. At every place was a glass of well-blended fruit cup, and out in the kitchen were great cakes being cut into generous slices, chocolate cake, fruit cake, coconut cake, sponge cake, pound cake, cupcakes, maple cake, custard cake, angel cake, and devil's food. It was a luscious array, and there were big freezers of ice cream.

But the two spies did not stop in the kitchen. The young officer cast a quick look about for three women who had been there an hour before. Finding them not, he went softly around, peering into little rooms that were used for Beginners and Primary Sunday school classes. At last in the farthest little room he found the three women kneeling in a corner.

"I thought so!" he said frowning, and wrote something in his little book.

"Now, come!" he said hurriedly. "There's a group of young people. I have to check up on them. They are here to wait on tables tonight and do some singing between the courses. They've given us a great deal of trouble this last year. They are comparatively new recruits, and such happy faces and joyous lives I've never seen. They've triumphed everywhere they've testified. We had to do something, so we've sowed dissent among them, turned their thoughts inward, showed them where they were being slighted, got them to see the faults of their friends. There was just no breaking up their fighting spirit before that, the way they were going on. They were meeting constantly to sing and pray, wearing radiant faces till everybody was asking why they were so happy. But we've had some of them on the run this last week. We'll see how they are tonight."

He pushed open a door that led into the church gymnasium, where stood about twenty young people in small groups, a girl and two boys, a boy and three girls, four or five girls. They were all talking earnestly, some of them emphatically. The two spies stepped near and listened.

"Well, she scarcely speaks to me anymore," a pleasant blonde girl with lovely wavy hair was saying.

"Why, Jeanette! I thought you all were wonderful friends. Wasn't it Mary and Fred who brought you to the Bible school in the first place?"

"Yes, it was," said Jeanette, her lip quivering, her eyes filling with sudden tears, "and we've always come together till two weeks ago. One night they just didn't come as usual, and they didn't send me any word, and when I met them the next morning they just nodded and never explained a thing. They haven't come to get me since, either! I waited for the bus that first night when I found they weren't coming, but it was late so I didn't go to class at all, and I've had to stay away ever since because the folks at home don't like me going all that long way in the dark to the bus."

"Well, I think Mary's jealous," said one of the girls earnestly. "I do, I really do! Fred's always so nice to all the girls."

"Well, he hasn't been nice these last two weeks," said Jeanette, turning away to hide her feelings. "But Mary couldn't have been jealous! She always sits with Fred in the front seat, and he always treats her as if she were the only person in the world, no matter how nice he is to us other girls."

"Oh, forget it, Jeanette," said one of the boys. "I guess Mary and Fred are out of fellowship. I heard they went off on a ride the other night instead of going to the meeting."

"Yes, Fred's going with those fellows down at the

Club again," sneered another lad. "I thought his conversion wouldn't last long."

The elder of the two spies lifted a satisfied face with a little smile hovering over his lips.

"They're all right!" he said. "There'll be more carnage tonight, if I don't miss my guess. Here, listen to these."

They drew near to another group of young people.

"What's the matter, Isabel? You haven't been coming down to the Bible class lately."

"Oh, well," laughed a pretty girl with a trifling beribboned Swiss apron over a frivolous dress, "I can't be bothered! What's the use anyway? I can't be good. I'm having too much fun. And since I found out that Tom Riley and his sisters go to dances, I don't see why I shouldn't have fun too. They're called such good Christians, and yet they do that! And I decided that probably every Christian is that way if you just knew. Awfully good Christians when they're leading a meeting, and do as they please the rest of the week!"

She laughed a mean little laugh.

"But you oughtn't to judge all Christians by what some do," protested a sweet, shy-looking girl, "and you oughtn't to judge Christ by what his poor, weak followers do!"

"Why not?" said Isabel sharply. "If he isn't able to make them different from other people as they sometimes claim, what good is it to be a Christian at all? Why not have a good time? Besides, I don't find any of them that don't say rotten things about some of the rest, and when I found that out I was done. I'll live my life the way I want to and I guess I'll come out as well as the rest." She laughed carelessly. "I just heard of a minister's wife who talks a lot of gossip about the different church members. I don't see that that is any better than going to dances. As far as I can see I'm as good as anybody."

"But, Isabel, you're missing a lot," pleaded the shy girl, "and the Lord *is* able to make his own children different. It's just that we don't let him have his way with us."

"I'm not missing anything I care about," said Isabel with a shrug of her shoulders. "Look at those two over there, Tom and Hullie. They went to meeting strong at first. Maybe they go now too, I don't know, but I just heard them telling Anna Sears the rottenest story ever about Greta Long, and she was one of those girls they used to pray for and take to meeting with them."

The senior spy smiled triumphantly toward the other.

"You see!" he said. "We've got them going. But what are those young people going into that little cloak room over there for? We must look into that."

He peered into a place where the paint had been scraped off the ground glass.

"Ah!" he said, drawing his breath sharply. "Another stronghold! That's one thing we can't work against!"

The apprentice, peering in after him, saw three young men and two girls down upon their knees praying earnestly that God would be in the midst of the meeting upstairs and overcome the evil one. "Have thy way with us all, Lord," they heard one say. "Take us and break us and make us over! Mold us, fill us all with thy Spirit *at any cost!*"

The older spy flashed an angry look.

"I must go at once and report this," he said. "Something strenuous will have to be done about it. Now there'll be reinforcements from angelic headquarters. It's those words 'at any cost' that destroy all our weapons. Come! This must be known at headquarters at once!" And the two slid silently out of the door and into the world of darkness.

Over the ramparts of heaven the angels leaned anxiously watching, while the professing church of God romped on "according to the course of this world, according to the prince of the power of the air, the spirit that now worketh in the children of disobedience." Having their conversation in the lusts of the flesh and not in the spirit, fulfilling the desires of the flesh and of the mind, just as though they were still by nature children of wrath and had not been quickened from their deadness in trespasses and sins.

The church was full that night, though many who belonged to the objecting contingent remained away. In fact almost every man who had held up the decisions in the afternoon by disagreement and opposition was conspicuously absent. Yet both galleries were packed. People even sat on the pulpit stairs and stood against the walls.

They didn't mind that the church organist was absent. A young man from a visiting church went to the piano and fairly made it speak the words as he played.

Mrs. Ridgeway sat in wonder until suddenly the young speaker caught her interest and her conscience with his first words:

"Therefore whatsoever ye have spoken in the darkness shall be heard in the light: and that which ye have spoken in the ear in closets shall be proclaimed upon the housetops."

Suddenly Mrs. Ridgeway remembered some of the things she had said about a lot of people that day, and she gave a tired shiver and decided it was time to go home. She was in no mood for heart-searching. She considered that she had done well that day and she didn't want to be made to suspect that perhaps she had not.

But a lot of people crowded into the seat just then, and she couldn't get out without making a disturbance, so she sat still and the speaker went on:

"For we are made a spectacle unto the world, and to angels, and to men."

In his opening sentences he spoke of the great world war and how the boys who went out to fight were under the eyes of the whole world. How each nation was watching them and weighing their value as soldiers.

"The Christian Church is in a warfare today!" he said. "Only our warfare is in the spirit realm, not in the natural, not against flesh and blood! The Christian has been delivered from the natural realm, delivered from self, good self, bad self, religious self, and all the other kinds of self; he has been brought into another sphere, and it is in that sphere he must live and wage his warfare.

"We have been hearing all day of the enemy, encamped upon the very outskirts of this lovely town. We have trembled to think what has been going on while we have been asleep to the danger. Now we are met together to combine our forces against the prince of the power of the air. One of the first things we need to realize is that we cannot make a single move without orders from on high, because we are not fighting just for Morningtown. We are fighting one of the battles in the great war against the enemy and we are a spectacle not only for the other towns about to see, the other states, the other nations, other men, but a spectacle for angels. They are watching us there on the ramparts of heaven. And Christian warfare in order to be effective must be fought from a heavenly standpoint, not from the earthly or carnal standpoint. And that being the case, we cannot use carnal weapons, that is, worldly weapons and devices such as human organization, and the businesslike schemes the world would use. If we do we are neglecting the spiritual and losing the power that is of God. There must be spiritual warfare on spiritual ground, with spiritual weapons, or else we are defeated at the start.

"We are here as a church to take the prey out of the hands of the evil one, that sinners may be saved, saints built up, and a people prepared for the coming of our Lord Jesus Christ in glory and power.

"The Holy Spirit begins instruction about this warfare by telling us what it is not, and one of the very first things he tells is that our warfare is not with one another! The very moment Christians get to warring with one another, the church is divided. We fall into criticism, sharpness, unforgiveness, and bitterness, and we are defeated. The very moment Christians get into a state of judging or criticizing, with bitterness and unforgiveness toward one another, they are not only defeated in their own lives, but other people are defeated by their influence. And by the things they do and say, the devil is well pleased. He knows very well that if he can get the church of God to warring with one another they will not war against him."

Mrs. Ridgeway's cheeks began to burn as she sat with bright eyes fixed upon the speaker, every word he spoke condemning her own actions.

For it was not only the things that Mrs. Ridgeway knew she had said that day about other Christians that were cutting like a knife into her conscience as she listened. Mrs. Ridgeway had a sister-in-law with whom she had been at war for years. A good Christian woman she was, too, and Mrs. Ridgeway knew it. Yet she had condemned almost everything she did, until she had worked her brother into a state of uneasiness that had almost broken up his household and his Christian testimony. And it had all started about some trifling differences of opinion until it had become a serious matter.

"I can tell you why your prayers are not answered!" said the speaker, "why you are not having the sweet experiences that God wants you to have. If as you analyze your life and experience you find any tendency to judge other people, to criticize, to speak evil of others, to have a bitter, unforgiving spirit, that is the cause. God will have to judge you if you criticize others.

"God wants you to go after sinners, to be loving and patient with saints, and if you are sharp and censorious with others you will only drive them away from God instead of winning them. God wants you to show forth by your life—even if you cannot say a word—that he has done something, that he has saved you and separated you unto himself, and given you his own life and his own patience and grace.

"There are many Christians who are worldly and who have no power in their lives. When you walk with God, and his Holy Spirit has his way with you, keeping you every step of the way, then he will give you power and answer your prayers. Put yourself into God's hands at any cost to yourself. Then he can make all this real to you. He has left you here on earth that his power might be manifested through you to others.

"When we are fighting among ourselves we cannot prove God's weapons mighty in pulling down the strongholds of the enemy. The enemy is watching. The angels are watching. The world is watching. 'By this shall all men know that ye are my disciples, if ye have love one toward another.' No, we've got to get a Calvary heart, the heart that made the Lord

Jesus willing to go to Calvary for men, before we can fight against the enemy's strongholds. You've got to love your fellow Christians even if they don't agree with you about a lot of things.

"Brethren of Morningtown, before you go out to battle, get down upon your knees and ask God to show you yourselves. Then examine your weapons. Be sure that they are not carnal weapons. Put on the whole armor of God, 'and above all, prayer.' Pray that there shall be no more divided battle. Then go forth and prove that God's spiritual weapons are mighty to the pulling down of strongholds. And remember that not only men and devils are watching you, but angels are watching also and rejoicing over your victories."

The noted speaker had to catch a train as soon as the service was over, but the audience was hard to disperse. People stood talking with one another and saying with tears in their eyes, "That was wonderful! That was what we needed. That hit home to me."

Everywhere, all over the church, people were confessing to one another, "That sermon was meant for me!" And here and there a couple who had not been speaking came together and shook hands. One or two asked forgiveness of one another.

Mrs. Ridgeway from her place high up in the gallery stood a moment or two and watched, and then hurried down and away into the night, going straight to her sister-in-law's house.

"I've come to tell you I've been wrong, Rebecca," she said, twisting wry lips and snapping the words out reluctantly. But there was a tear in her eye, and Rebecca saw something more like humility in her face than had ever been there before.

Back at church a group dropped down upon their knees up near the pulpit, and began to pray, and others who had been standing in the aisles or by the door tiptoed up and knelt beside them. Incense of prayer arose as a sweet-smelling savor to the Lord, prayer that could be answered. Humble, contrite prayer, prayer that was filled with confession of sin. The kind of prayer that took hold upon the promises of God.

Then in a panic the listeners in the shadows fled. These Christians had forgotten their differences and had begun to pray! The battle was on and the God of battles was in command! It mattered not that the three most influential churches in Morningtown were not represented in that group upon their knees. The angels were not counting riches nor influence nor education. They were looking upon those who were utterly yielded to their God and ready to go to the forefront of battle with him.

Reinforced from above, Curtius Goodwin and his helpers went forward to the battle, fortified by constant prayer.

They did not draw up any finely worded petitions against the evils in the town, nor get up crusades. They were not fighting with carnal weapons. They did not even canvass the town to get voters against the gangsters. They established a prayer room in the corner of the great old tabernacle they had repaired and refurnished, and prayer was sent up continually, day and night.

"But I don't understand," said Dr. Patton one day, meeting Mr. Tupper on the street. "You made such a stir about how you were going to fight the enemy, and you haven't closed up one notorious place yet."

"No," said Mr. Tupper radiantly. "No, brother, we haven't bothered about cleaning up the places. The places are only the result of sin and lost souls. We are trying to save the souls. Had you heard yet, Brother Patton, that Dirk Sullivan was saved last night? Dirk, you know, is the proprietor of the most notorious gambling den in Morningtown, and Dirk is *saved!* That means that one gambling den at least is finished!"

"Saved?" said the good doctor raising his eyebrows. "Now, just what do you mean by the expression, Brother Tupper? You mean he has got emotional and come forward in your meeting? But how long will it last?"

"As long as eternity lasts!" said Mr. Tupper joyously. "No, Dirk didn't come forward. We didn't even know he had been to the meetings. He came quietly one night at midnight to talk with the evangelist who had been preaching that evening—" Mr. Tupper did not remember that it was the noted evangelist to whom Dr. Patton personally had objected in that first meeting, but Dr. Patton did, and winced a little—"and he told him he felt that he was a great sinner and he needed a Savior, but he couldn't believe that Christ had died for such as he. Then after the way had been made plain to him, Dirk Sullivan got down on his knees and prayed, and he told the Lord that his gambling den would never be open again. I went down there with the evangelist this morning and found him as good as his word. The gambling equipment was being burned, and the place scrubbed clean. He wants some of the young people to come down there tonight and hold a prayer meeting. He's bought some chairs and hymn books himself, and he wants to bring Christ where he formerly served the devil, he says."

"You don't say!" said Dr. Patton, rubbing away the mist that had come to his eyes. "You *don't say!* Well, I hope he sticks!"

But the angels were gazing in wonder at the manifold wisdom and grace of God.

THE STRANGE GOD

THE Brandons had always been active Christian workers even when they were very young. Frank Brandon had been made president of the Christian Endeavor in his church when he was a mere boy; and Emily Fuller of the Epworth League in her church when she was very young. Both of them had sung in the choir, both had been most zealous in county and district work of all sorts. They were always being put on committees either in church or community work, wherever any activity was started along religious lines. Just as soon as anything was decided upon, someone would always say, "We'll get Frank Brandon interested in that and it will be sure to go like wildfire," or, "Put Emily Fuller in charge of that and there won't be a hitch in your arrangements."

And so when these two joined forces in marriage, everyone was marveling over their future, and the respective Fuller and Brandon contingents each began planning to absorb them both.

This of course was most pleasant and flattering to

them, and the result was that finally each took over many of the activities of the other, and became busier than ever, abounding in good works, with scarcely time to call their souls their own. But they seemed to enjoy it. They continued to take on new activities until one wondered how they did it. But they never complained of being weary. They seemed to thrive on the adulation of their friends.

"Oh, you two! You're simply tireless, aren't you?" an elderly member would say, shaking an admiring finger at Emily playfully, and sighing lazily. "You'll certainly have a lot of stars in your crown! I wish I were as good a Christian as you are! You'll certainly have your reward in heaven! How *do* you *do* it?"

"Oh, that's nothing!" Emily would say lightly, "I just love this kind of work. But, dear Mrs. Brown, *are* you going to make us one of your marvelous angel cakes for the sale? And *would* it be too much to ask for two quarts of your celestial salad besides? You know, if your name is on anything we can charge half again as much and get away with it. We do want to make enough to get a new church carpet. The old one is simply unspeakable!"

Mrs. Brown would always end by promising both angel cake and salad, and patting Emily on her exquisitely rouged cheek, saying, "What a wonderful little Christian you always were, Emily; I quite envy you your crown!" And Emily would dimple and smile and flutter across the aisle to beg Mrs. Peters for four quarts of her "heavenly mayonnaise" to put in little amber jars with her name hand-painted on the label.

It was just the same with Frank. "Frank, old man, we're putting on a comedy to help out with the mortgage on the church this year, and we want you for end man. Now there's no use in making excuses, for there's nobody who can put over the jokes the way you can, and we mean to have you."

Or the Sunday school superintendent would accost him. "Brandon, how about your taking that class of boys? They've had five teachers and finished them all, and the one they have now isn't a teacher at all. He just sits and lets them walk all over him. You could manage them, I'm sure. Get them interested in some class activity; basketball, or tennis, or something athletic, and make them feel some church responsibility. They can join the church leagues and play with other churches, win cups and things, that'll give them a church spirit! Why, those fellows ought all to be church members at their age! How'd it be if you make a rule that only church members are eligible to play in the interchurch games? Something like that, see? I'm sure you'd be just the one to start it."

"Good idea!" said Frank pleasantly. "I'm not sure, but I'd enjoy that if I can make the time. I can see possibilities. We could have weekend conferences in the summer up at one of the camps and teach them the latest methods of church work; raising money, etc., and give them a dash of church history, or maybe a talk or two on personal responsibility; something really serious. Then when they get home let them put on a church social, using some of the methods they've learned. We could give two or three prizes; one for the most original program, one for the best suggestion of how to raise money for the church, and—well—one for the best menu for a church banquet. Yes, I can see great possibilities. I'll think it over and try to make time for it. It sounds great to me!"

Things had been going on like this for several years. Frank had a great Bible class of boys—very many boys and very little Bible; and Emily had a like class of girls, whose chief business it was to get up new and startling ways of entertainment to hold the boys in the church. Visiting strangers, introduced to the Brandons and informed how wonderful they were, would respond with a wistful wish that they had some such workers in their church.

The church the Brandons attended was the most thoroughly programmed of any church in the city. The minister was wont to boast that the young people of his church had no need to go anywhere else for their entertainment, they had enough at home.

"Sorry, brother," Frank Brandon said when Harry Sharpless, an earnest young man from another church who was formerly a member of Frank's Bible class, suggested their joining in a city-wide movement for weekly Bible study. "Sorry, but we wouldn't have time to spare. Monday and Thursday nights we have our regular league games; Wednesday night we have practice in our own church gym. Of course that doesn't come till after the prayer meeting, but it breaks into the evening and no one would like taking on another date, for we require them to be on time at practice. Of course, the young people don't go to prayer meeting. But to tell the truth, some of them get into the gym while prayer meeting is going on and have a little practice on the side, so that hour wouldn't be available. Then Tuesday night our church orchestra and choirs meet, and a lot of our young folks belong to those. Friday night we have either movies or some kind of church entertainment, and Saturday nights we have our church "Get Together Club." Ever hear about that? It's quite unique. We have the whole church divided into sections and they take turns being hosts and hostesses. We have a supper connected with it, of course. We've just put in a miniature golf course in the basement of the church. The young people did the work themselves, and it's great! The old people sit around the fire and sing popular songs and the young folks play games. We have a couple of ping pong tables too. It's really great. Ever been over to see it? You ought to come. Of course we have a modest charge for outsiders to come and play. But I'd be glad to have you come as my guest sometime. You'd enjoy it and maybe get an idea of how to work something like it in your church. No, I'm sorry, Harry. I'm afraid we wouldn't be able to join you in that Bible study idea. And, you see, we really don't need it. Our young people are all hard at work in the church, and of course most of them come from Christian homes and we get plenty of that sort of thing on Sunday anyway."

It was the winter that they were putting on the missionary play that Emily stopped Rose Altar, a newcomer to the church, and asked her to come to a committee meeting that was to be held in the church parlor an hour before the morning session of Sunday school next Sunday.

"I'm sorry," said Rose, "I'm afraid I couldn't come at that time. You see, we always have family worship at that hour. Sometimes during the week we have to be hurried, but Father likes to take more time for it on Sundays."

"Family worship! How quaint!" said Emily, staring a little. "Imagine it! I didn't know anybody did that anymore. But couldn't you stay away just once? You see, we're putting on a marvelous play next month and we're assigning the characters. We want to begin to rehearse this week because we want to take all the time possible for preparation, and we thought we could just read over some of the parts and let you get the idea, and see what you were expected to do. We'd do it in the afternoon, only the church orchestra is giving a sacred concert then and a good many of us are in that. But anyhow, can't you come just this once? Tell your father it's *quite* religious. It's a sort of a pageant of all missionary lands. The costumes are gorgeous! They are ordered from abroad. The Mission Board is getting them for us. There's a dear little Mohammedan one that I think would about fit you. I know you would be stunning in it. We are hoping to do a lot of good with this play. It's the beginning of the great World Drive for Foreign Missions, you know, and it's marvelous what a prospect we have. We've already had three invitations to put the play on at other churches. If all goes well we rather expect to give it a good many times, in the suburbs, and even over in the next state. I wanted to be sure and get you to come in with us right at the start, for I have an idea you'll be awfully good."

But Rose Altar shook her head.

"I'm sorry, Mrs. Brandon; you're very kind, but I just haven't time for things of that sort."

"Oh, I'm sorry," said Emily a bit shortly.

She was stung and astonished that the sweet young stranger had not immediately recognized and followed her lead. She was not used to having anyone refuse her requests and invitations.

"Poor child," she said to herself, looking after her with an almost contemptuous smile. "She must be under the domination of a fanatical father. Fancy family worship! How quaint! How Victorian! Well, she'll come around, of course, when she sees it's the thing to do; but she'll have to take what is left. I can't run any risks waiting. She can be a Zulu girl, of course, if nothing else is left, though she may object to the bead costumes. However—I've done my best for her."

So the play went on and enthusiasm spread like wildfire.

The Bible study classes went on also, and many unexpected ones were added to them—of such as should be saved. But there was a large number of eager, earnest young church members who would have come into the Bible meetings and enjoyed them, but they felt their first duty was toward the mission play that their own church was getting up. It was going to do so much good for foreign missions!

Frank Brandon, coming home from his office an hour later than usual one day in late February, swung himself aboard the train just as it was starting, and walked through three crowded cars, finally dropping into the only vacant seat he could find, the little single one by the door. He opened the evening paper. He was extremely tired and didn't want to talk, for things had not gone well. The first thing that morning his valued secretary had sent word that her mother was very sick and she couldn't come to the office that day. He had been obliged to hire a public stenographer. Then about ten o'clock word had come that the bank where he kept his prosperous account had closed its doors, cutting him off indefinitely, not only from his bank account, but also from the safety deposit box, which contained valuable papers and bonds which might be used for collateral. Besides, he had a headache and a sore throat and ached all over. His throat had been sore when he left home that morning in the sleet and slush, having forgotten his rubbers in his haste. He shivered as the draught from the opening and closing car door slithered down his collar. He felt miserably sick and remembered he had a meeting of the federated committees in the church that evening. He unfurled a newspaper more as a protection than because he wanted to read it. He didn't want to talk to anyone. He was not noticing his fellow passengers. His eyes were on his paper, though he was not much interested in its news. The usual number of accidents, murder cases, and a new suicide—Mather, director of the bank where his money had been. Well, what good did that do, committing suicide? Coward! Thinking to slip out of his obligations that way and leave the mess to other people! Well, of course the man wasn't even a church member. He hadn't any respect for himself. You couldn't expect a man like that—

Suddenly he forgot to finish his thought, for he heard his own name spoken by one of the two men sitting just in front of him. He hadn't noticed who they were, but now he recognized their voices. One was Mr. Harris, a successful lawyer, as noted for his interest in church affairs, as he was in his profession. The other was Harry Sharpless. It was Harris who spoke first:

"Did that man Brandon from the Fifth Church go into your Bible conference work?"

"No," said the other, "he said he hadn't time!"

"Why, I'm surprised," said Harris. "I supposed he was a live wire, always interested in church affairs. With such speakers and teachers as you have secured I would have expected him to *take* the time!"

"Haven't you ever noticed," said young Sharpless with a bit of a twinkle, "that Frank Brandon never goes in for anything that he himself isn't running? He just has to be the head or he won't play. And from all I've seen his wife must be a good deal the same way. It's a case of:

I love me! I love me!
I'm wild about myself!

I love me! I love me!
My picture's on my shelf!"

"Well, I don't know about that," said the graver voice sadly. "I hadn't thought about it before. Too bad, isn't it? He could be such a power. Do you know, Sharpless, there are a great many self-worshipers today who are going about most actively carrying on service in their own strength, and for their own sakes. They worship self under the impression that they are worshiping God. That is the blinding of the enemy, a part of the great delusion. Power, success, without God! When all the time the Lord is saying: 'Not by might, nor by power, but by my spirit, saith the Lord of hosts!'

"What a pity Brandon couldn't be present at some of those meetings. Even one would be an eye-opener to him, for I believe that at heart he is a conscientious young man, if he could only be made to see the truth."

Frank Brandon shrank further behind his paper. Cold angry chills ran down his back, and a sick feeling came into the pit of his stomach. His feet and hands were like ice and his face burned hot with fury. Was this what people thought of him? Was it possible that they so misjudged him? Admired and successful though he had been, generous and ready to help everybody, yet there were those who thought of him like that! Of course it was jealousy. A man couldn't expect to be popular and not have some people jealous of him. But these were Christian people, prominent in church circles! Who would ever have suspected them of such petty jealousy? Well, he was thankful that he had none of that! A scrap from the solo he had sung in church last Sunday rang through his memory:

God, I thank thee that I am not as other men!
I fast twice in the week,
I give tithes of all that I possess!

And they thought he was an egotist! Both of them actually agreed that he was always thinking of himself. That obnoxious song that Sharpless had quoted! He knew it. He used to sing it in college. His lips shut sternly. It was outrageous!

Well, he would just forget it, of course; that was the Christian thing to do. But somehow he must show those two that what they said was untrue. He really couldn't stand having anybody going around talking about him like that! Perhaps it would be a good thing to just lean over and challenge what they had said now, settle the matter right then and there and dominate the situation before those two went out and spread such an idea! That was the only way to handle such a thing. Prove them in the wrong, embarrass them, just lean forward and smile and ask them pleasantly—well—just what could he ask them? He couldn't merely get up and declare himself innocent of their charge. If they really had such a thing in the back of their minds, his word that it wasn't so wouldn't mean a thing. What proof could he bring that it wasn't so?

Then like a tantalizing little imp, the couplet ran through his brain.

I love me! I love me!
I'm wild about myself.

And something moved within him. Could it be that there was any truth in the assertion that he wasn't interested in anything that he himself didn't run? Of course people were always asking him to take over the management of so many things. He couldn't help it, could he, that there were so many things he was responsible for that he hadn't time for the rest? There! That was something he could ask those two! He would do it right away and see what they said.

But having made this resolve he suddenly felt that he must have a little more to say.

While he paused to collect a list of his good works wherewith to confound them, suddenly the two rose as one man, with the exclamation: "Why, there is Dr. Leveridge up there at the other end of the car. Let's go and speak to him!" and they hurried eagerly forward to greet a gray-haired, kindly faced man. Frank recognized him as one who had been pointed out to him a few days ago as a conference speaker.

Frank lowered his paper an inch and watched the eager meeting between the three men. He saw how their faces lighted. He was wont to see faces lighted with greeting like that for himself. Yet two of these faces held behind them thoughts against his reputation as a Christian! Of course Sharpless had been just a kid in his Sunday school class not long ago.

But a sick wave of fury passed over him. Somehow he felt left out, and he was not used to being left out.

He couldn't just march down the aisle and tell them he had overheard them talking about him. They hadn't even known he was there! But he could easily get out into the other car now while they were up front and they would never know he had been there. That was of course the dignified thing to do, and he had known it all the time, only his fury had made him impatient. He would go at once while they had their backs turned. He arose swiftly and slipped out the door, crossing the platform to the next car.

There were no seats in the next car and Frank had to stand on the platform by the door, swaying with the train and hiding his face with his newspaper. But it was a salve to his hurt feelings to know that there were several younger men in that aisle ahead of him who would eagerly have urged him to take their seats while they stood in the aisle or sat on the arm, hanging on his words, if they had known he was there. But he was not ready to talk with anyone just now. He had just received the shock of his life. It had never before entered his head that any one *could* talk that way about him. He felt a righteous wrath, with a great pity for himself, and felt he must get himself adjusted and decide what to do before he talked with anyone, even Emily.

He decided not to tell Emily anything about it. No need of her having to bear this, too. Of course young Sharpless had been the only one of the two who had said anything really mean. That awful song—"I love me!" It disgusted him more and more as he thought of it. What Lawyer Harris had said wasn't so bad, only he had in a way accepted the slur. Christian people! Talking that way about one who was doing twice as much Christian work as they were!

Well, somehow he must prove to them that they were wrong. How would it do to go to one of their old meetings? Let himself be seen in a front seat! Make it known that he was in thorough sympathy, only he had not been able to go sooner! That was a good idea. If he could get rid of this rotten headache and the aches all over him, he would go tonight. Of course there was a meeting of the federated committees tonight, but it wasn't important, and he could telephone to Sommers to take his place as chairman for once. Well, he would do it no matter how bad he felt! It was important to reverse this feeling before everyone heard of it.

When the train stopped at his station he swung off into the darkness, hurrying down the street to his home. He didn't take a taxi lest someone else would be in it. He didn't want to talk with anyone. His throat was raw and his head throbbing. He drew his collar up about his neck and bent his head against the wind and sleet. He knew he was in no condition to go out again that night, but he meant to go. It rather gave him satisfaction that he was going in spite of being sick. It had come to seem quite the most important thing in the world that he be seen in the front seat of the conference *at once*.

At home Emily protested, "Why, you are *sick*, Frank, and it's beginning to sleet! You're not fit to go out. Besides, you have that committee meeting. I was going to suggest that you call them up and have them meet here. Then we could ask their wives and serve coffee and cake afterward. I think that would be much more interesting."

"No," said Frank, "I've got to go to that conference tonight! I promised I'd look in on them, and this is perhaps the last night! Anyhow, it's important. There are reasons why I feel that I should lend my influence to it. And I'd like you to go along with me if possible! I really feel we ought! I find it's quite expected of us, and I guess it must be a good thing. They need encouragement. Poor things. They've got that great hall on their hands and I don't suppose it'll be half filled. We really should have gone earlier, taken hold of the thing somehow. It seems people think *we* ought to do *everything!*"

So they went to the meeting. When they turned into the street where the hall was located they wondered if there was a funeral somewhere, there were so many cars parked on both sides of the street. They had to go a block and a half away from the hall and walk back, and Frank had forgotten his rubbers again.

When they reached the hall, they were surprised to find people pouring in by the hundreds. They thought at first they must have gotten into the wrong place.

And there was no front seat to be had! Indeed there was scarcely a seat left anywhere on the street floor, and the galleries were filling fast. Men were already standing leaning against the walls. So Frank found a place for Emily behind a post where practically no one could see her, while he stalked up the aisle and took up his stand on his angry aching limbs at one side of the pulpit steps. He leaned against the cold, cold wall, and presently discovered there was a cold air ventilator right over his head that blew down his neck. But anyone who could see the platform could not fail to see him standing there, one foot braced on the lower step of the pulpit. There he stood with a haughty heart but a smile of patronage locked upon his face for the evening.

It was hard work standing there with his whole body aching like a toothache. The room was hot, for the audience was vast, and he was constantly conscious of his hot, dry, prickly throat. But as he gazed into the faces of that audience he forgot his own discomforts. In amazement he noticed people present who seldom attended any church. He wondered how they got them there? There hadn't been any special advertising! And there were familes, *whole* families, from all the churches, eagerly uniting in singing with a zest that showed they counted it a special privilege to be there. This really was something that he ought to have recognized, it seemed. Yet failing to find a response from him, the Lord had done it without him! He felt somehow aggrieved at God.

The singing astonished him right at the start; it was so tremendous, and the congregation didn't need to be worked up to it, either. There was an earnest man up on the platform holding them all in perfect time with an unobstrusive hand. He had a cultured voice with heartthrobs in its very timbre, but he seemed to be merely directing the great volume of sound that was not perfunctory, but came from hearts alive and singing unto the Lord.

Frank Brandon had conducted choruses himself that had been considered great successes. He had always felt he could bring out of an audience the utmost sound it possessed. But he had never heard such singing as this in his life. As they started on the second hymn, which was eagerly requested from the audience, he found there were tears in his eyes. But the words were almost startling. They were:

Empty me of self, Lord Jesus—

He looked around furtively, half wondering if Sharpless or Harris had called for it. He felt once more that sharp stab of query. *Was* he a self-willed man without knowing it?

The tide of song swept him, thrilling him with its greatness, and bringing a strange wistfulness that he might have been a part of all this from its inception. Then with his newly awakened senses, he questioned keenly, was that pang he felt jealousy? He put that aside to think about later, for a man with a marvelous voice was singing a solo, not merely showing off his glorious voice, but singing a message to souls:

Not I, but Christ, be honored, loved, exalted;
Not I, but Christ, be seen, be known, be heard;
Not I, but Christ, in every look and action,
Not I, but Christ, in every thought and word.

Christ, only Christ, no idol ever falling;
Christ, only Christ, no needless bustling sound;
Christ, only Christ, no self-important bearing;
Christ, only Christ, no trace of "I" be found.

O to be saved from myself, dear Lord,
O to be lost in Thee,
O that it might be no more I,
But Christ, that lives in me.

The words sank deep into his soul, and added to his discomfort. Up there in the shadows of the vaulted ceiling, somewhere above the gallery, he seemed to feel a Presence whose eyes were searching him through and through!

But the voice of the preacher broke in upon his thoughts. It was the Dr. Leveridge whom Harry Sharpless and Lawyer Harris had met so eagerly on the train! Frank looked up, prejudiced against him already, and studied the kind, strong face, the fine head crowned with silver hair, the keen eyes. But in spite of his prejudice he could not but admire the cultured voice of the speaker as he announced his text:

"If we have forgotten the name of our God, or stretched out our hands to a strange god; shall not God search this out? for he knoweth the secrets of the heart."

The verse was utterly unfamiliar to Frank Brandon and startled him as if the words had been spoken for him alone. It reached even to joints and marrow and divided the very soul and spirit of him. It seemed to Frank Brandon that he had never heard a verse of Scripture before that so searched his being. He wondered in his astonishment where the preacher had found such a verse. He did not remember having heard it before. Some new translation, probably! But it gave him for the first time in his life the consciousness of God searching out his innermost secrets. God right there looking into his thoughts! A great panic swept over him, causing him to doubt whether God would really find everything in him entirely satisfactory. Was he, after all, quite as letter-perfect as he had always supposed himself? This sudden amazing jolt to his usually complacent spirit, added to the discomfort of his body, made his situation almost unbearable. He indignantly put away such thoughts and set his lips to smile approbation. His whole attitude and expression ought to show keen interest and enjoyment. He must carry this through to the end at all odds.

The preacher swept on with a discourse that burned into his soul with a new kind of torture. He began by speaking of things that go toward making a soul forget God. Prominent in the list, he mentioned great Christian activity, especially the kind in which men make a plan and ask God to bless it, rather than waiting on the Lord to discover what he would have done. He tore the halo from the Christian who is immersed in this sort of man-planned activity by holding up to view a Lord whose very love constrains the heart to look to him and "lean not to its own understanding."

Frank Brandon listened in amazement to a doctrine he had never heard even hinted at before. He knew in his honest heart that nearly everything that he had ever done in the name of Christ had been after this sort, and if this were true he was being condemned. He tried to reason against it all, to protest in his soul, but the preacher was backing up every word he said with a verse of Scripture.

Then the preacher went on to speak of strange gods that men commonly set up in their souls. Money, pleasure, worldly amusement, fleshly lust—

Ah! Frank lifted up his head triumphantly. None of these were enshrined in his heart. Of that he was very sure. He had lived a clean life, he had no time for worldly amusement, or personal pleasure, and he was not especially fond of money. Look how well he had behaved that morning when the bank closed! He had always given largely of what he possessed. He did not feel condemned in any of those ways.

But now the speaker had come to another god, the commonest one, he said, the one most often enshrined in the human heart. That was Self. Self-will, self-esteem, having one's own way, the desire to dominate, even over God himself, and bend his way to our will.

He went into the matter most fully and keenly. Like a surgeon using the scalpel of the Word of God, he laid bare Frank Brandon's true self to his own eyes. He saw himself by his very activities putting God out and himself in, getting praise to himself instead of God; actually singing praises to himself. That heathenish little verse flashed through his harried mind.

I love me! I love me!
I'm wild about myself!

He began to see that his very attendance tonight at this strange meeting had been for the worship of self, an attempt to put self back on its pedestal before the world.

In closing the speaker brought out the fact that this self-worship was the sin of Satan who once was Lucifer, son of the morning, the anointed cherub, until iniquity was found in him. Satan's sin was in trying to put himself in God's place. The speaker quoted the awful condemnation:

How art thou fallen from heaven, O Lucifer, son of the morning! how art thou cut down to the ground, which didst weaken the nations!
For thou hast said in thine heart, I will ascend into heaven, I will exalt my throne above the stars of God: I will sit also upon the mount of the congregation, in the sides of the north:
I will ascend above the heights of the clouds; I will be like the most High.
Yet thou shalt be brought down to hell, to the sides of the pit!

From then on Frank Brandon was engrossed in his task of heart-searching until they began to sing in closing that hymn of consecration:

Have thine own way, Lord! Have thine own way!
Thou art the Potter, I am the clay.
Mold me and make me after thy will,
While I am waiting yielded and still.

He knew those words. He had taught them to many an audience. He had always urged them not to drag. "Make it snappy!" he used to say. Never before had the words meant a thing to him. Now they thrilled through him like an alien prayer in which his lips were forced to join, but his soul was full of wild rebellion, struggling to keep self on its shrine.

He did the proper thing at the close of the meeting: shook hands with the preacher and those active in the conference; told them how sorry he was that his other dates had prohibited his being present at every session, said how wonderful the meeting had been, and how much he knew he had missed; told them to count on him for anything he could do to keep up the spirit of the conference; explained how he was president of this, chairman of that, leader of the other, his time so filled that he could scarcely ever do anything extra. And then suddenly he realized that nobody was listening to him. Nobody seemed to have noticed his absence nor to be especially delighted that he was here tonight. They seemed to take it for granted that anybody would be there who could!

Finally, with a sick sense that he could not stand much more and ought to be in bed, he found Emily behind her post and hurried home.

Sometime in the night he awoke to the knowledge that he was very ill indeed. His body was on fire with fever and yet shivering with cold. His eyes were burning, his head was throbbing, his limbs aching unbearably, and his throat swollen almost shut.

Emily was up doing things for him, asking him wearisome questions that he did not want to answer. There were hot-water bags about him and an ice bag on his head. A doctor was there somewhere in the dimness of things. Was that possibly a nurse in the offing? And Emily beside the bed on her knees sobbing—it might even be praying.

It all wearied him inexpressibly and he wandered off into a strange place of fire and ice. He did not want to go but it seemed some duty was compelling him; and then he saw before him shrines, his and Emily's. They were like two wooden alcoves on the clear icy pavement, with shelves above a kneeling place, and pictures in costly frames upon the shelves, and haloes over the pictures. He stepped closer to see the picture in his own shrine and found it was a likeness of himself! He was startled to notice what a proud and haughty expression he wore, hard, worldly! Was he like that? And did God search it out and see it? He looked again and now he saw there was sin in his face. Actual sin!

Heartsick, he stepped aside to see what picture was in Emily's shrine, and lo, it was not her own likeness that was there, but another picture of his own haughty self with a self-satisfied smile upon his face. He wondered in his fevered brain whether in the eyes of God it was any better for a woman to have her husband in God's place rather than herself? He dimly perceived that they were both strange gods in the eyes of God. Then somehow there seemed to be a compelling force upon him that made it necessary for him to go back to his own shrine and worship. Pray to himself! How could he?

Ah, there were prayers stored up upon the shelf—many of them! High-sounding words full of fleshly desires, ending always: "Bless *my*self, *my* work, make all *my* schemes succeed and *my* enemies fail." They seemed so empty now as he took them down and read them over painfully upon his knees.

And now a song of praise to his strange god was required of him, and there was only one song he knew. His voice suddenly shrilled out through the sick room, startling the nurse and Emily as they hovered anxiously near at hand. It wasn't the voice wherewith he had charmed audiences with wonderful solos, nor yet the rich tones wherewith he had carried audiences into great tides of song. It was a high, excited, fevered voice shrilling and breaking and fading into nothing.

I love me! I love me!
I'm wild about myself!

"Oh Frank! *Don't! Please* don't!" sobbed Emily, very far away.

"But I *must,* Emily," he protested petulantly. "Don't you see the picture there on my shelf? I *have* to sing."

I love me! I love me!
There's my picture-on-my-shelf!

His voice suddenly trailed away into silence.

Then he looked up at the picture and saw an astonishing thing. For now the picture, though himself unmistakably, nevertheless had the evil, handsome eyes of Lucifer, son of the morning, and he saw even out of the murk of his delirium that "whoso putteth himself in the place of God" is really putting there Satan, the tempter of the world, the enemy of

God, the enemy of the Savior of the world. And suddenly Frank Brandon knew himself to be a sinner and cried aloud in awful anguish!

"Oh *God!* Forgive! Help! *Help!*"

The nurse thought that he was in pain and gave him a soothing powder till he slept.

But Emily upon her knees beside the bed was praying! She thought that he was dying, and she prayed, *really* prayed, perhaps for the first time in her life.

A long time afterward he awoke in the dim quiet of the sick room. Emily and the nurse were hovering in silence not far away, awaiting the outcome.

Suddenly the hush of the room was broken once more by song.

It was still not the voice with which he used to charm audiences or conduct choruses so successfully. It was not even the voice with which he had sung that strange grotesque melody when he was taken sick, or the voice with which he had cried out to God for mercy when he saw himself and his own sin. It was a thin, high thread of a voice, burned out with fever, and quavering with weakness.

Oh—to—be—saved from myself—*dear Lord!*
  Oh—to—be—lost in Thee!
Oh—that it might be—no—more—*I,*
  But Christ—*that lives—in—me!*

At the first breath Emily crept to his side and knelt, slipping her hand into the thin white hand that lay so feebly on the coverlet. But the feeble fingers held her own in a weak pressure, and the shadow of a smile trembled over his lips as he said faintly, pausing for breath:

"Isn't that what we want it to be, dear—from—now—on? *Christ—in—us?*"

"Oh, yes," she answered softly, "just his will! Frank, dearest, do you know, it was not until I handed you over to him, and prayed, 'Not my will, but thine be done,' that he gave you back to me, and you began to get better."

It was very quiet in the room, while a soft understanding passed from one hand to the other, and then tenderly two voices instead of one quavered out into the silence again.

Have thine own way, Lord, have thine own way!
Hold o'er my being absolute sway!
Fill with thy Spirit till all shall see
Christ only, always, living in me!

The nurse was standing just outside the door listening to see if she would be needed, and now she turned away with a strange mistiness in her eyes, saying softly to herself:

"Well, those two must have been real, after all! I didn't think they were!"

THE LOST MESSAGE

THE Rev. John Tresevant sat in his well-appointed study on Saturday morning at nine-thirty, trying to bring his mind down to writing a sermon for the next day.

He had just returned from his vacation, a cruise on the luxurious yacht of a wealthy parishioner, Elliot Rand. He had expected to come back not only renewed in physical energy, but with his mind full of new, vigorous ideas for sermons and full preparation for at least two Sundays ahead.

But he had not found the atmosphere of the yacht conducive to thought or work. There had been many lively guests on board, and he was expected to enter into all the gaiety of the lazy days, on a smooth sea under a blue sky. The moonlit nights were spent in the company of people who neither knew nor cared anything about theology. Also the cruise had been prolonged four days beyond the original time planned, so that this was the very last day before the minister's vacation ended. And he had nothing prepared for the morrow. It was imperative that he work hard all day, and he never felt less like work.

The telephone did its part in hindering. It rang incessantly. Mrs. Brown had broken her leg, and longed to see her pastor. She was the wife of another prominent member of his session. Her wishes were law. Mr. Addison was in the hospital with pneumonia and not expected to live from hour to hour. Mrs. Addison was the president of the Ladies' Aid, and most efficient, and she had been telephoning for three days for attendance from her pastor. Old Mrs. Hargraves was dead and the funeral must be arranged for, the family visited. Mrs. Barker had just been taken to the insane asylum and her husband had asked that the pastor call as soon as possible.

He was beginning to get desperate. He had started just one sentence on the smooth, expensive paper that lay before him, and he wasn't quite sure whether he was pleased with it or not.

Again the telephone rang.

He turned his annoyed glance toward the innocent little black instrument of torture and reached out his hand to the receiver.

"Yes?"

That tone of his was perfect. It could easily rise into wrath or soothe into honeyed tones, according to the status of the intruder. Much practice had made it a marvel of its kind.

And then it was only his wife, Elaine! Elaine, who knew just what he had to do, and what interruptions meant to him, to be so thoughtless as to call him from the country club where he knew she had gone that morning to play golf! It was too annoying!

"My *dear!*" His tone indicated that she was anything but dear at that moment.

"Now, you needn't get cross, John," said Elaine's honeyed tones. "I'm not calling on my own initiative. It's Elliot Rand who wants you. He has some people here; he wants to have them meet you. They have slews of moncy and they are just looking for a place to put it. He says they would just as soon as not put it into some marvelous stained glass windows for our new church if they happen to like you. He wants you to come down at once and play in a foursome with them. I'm taking the women to lunch at the club, and you've simply *got* to come!"

"But—my *dear!*" The tone was accusatory. "My sermons—!"

"Yes, I told him, John, that you had to work. I made it as strong as I could, but he said this was more important than any sermons, and that it didn't matter what you preached, you could just preach some old sermon over again and the people would never know! He said anyway that you simply *must* come!"

"I don't see how I possibly can—" began John Tresevant. "Mrs. Hargraves is dead and Mr. Addison may be dying of pneumonia—"

"Well, you can't bring Mrs. Hargraves to life, nor keep Mr. Addison from dying," said Elaine in a sweet, irresponsible voice, "and Elliot Rand *wants* you, so you know what you have to do! Put on your white flannel suit. It's in your closet. The tailor just brought it back this morning. I'll tell Jasper to get out your golf clubs and have them ready, and I'll drive back and get you. Hurry. They want to start playing at once! Wear that blue tie I bought you, the one that matches your eyes, you know. It's in the upper drawer of your chiffonier."

In the end, of course, he went. He had known from the first that he would have to. He hung up with a despairing look at that one sentence, not yet completed: "The trouble with the world today is—"

Would it be possible for him to do some thinking about his theme while he was playing golf? What was his theme, anyway, and was there a text that would be apt in connection with this thought?

While he hastily put on the white flannels and the blue tie according to instructions, he was threshing his brains and trying to get an inspiration. Surely, surely his fertile brain would not play him false. He had of late gained great confidence in himself. If worse came to worst he could surely extemporize—just look up three or four good illustrations and build something around them. He had always been a ready speaker. But that was not what he had wanted to do that first Sunday after his return from vacation. He had wanted to preach something that would impress not only the church, but the public press, the city of admirers and adherents. He had made a reputation for wise sayings, and deep intellectual addresses that were called "profound," and "challenging," and "epoch-revealing" according to the degree of education and imagination of the various press reporters, and he wanted to keep it up. Especially at the start of a new season, he wanted to do something really brilliant, and to do him justice he was filled with panic to think how little time he had in which to achieve this great end.

If he went to the country club he couldn't hope to get away until afternoon at best. And yet, as Elaine had stated, it was Elliot Rand who had asked it, so he must go. Elliot Rand simply owned the church. Whatever he wanted must be done, or the flow of money would stop. Elliot Rand had ways of looking coldly at anyone who dared to differ from him in the slightest degree. Elliot Rand had to be pleased at any cost.

The day was deliriously lovely, and the golf course perfect. The Mr. Clinton whom Elliot Rand desired to please out of some money for stained glass windows was a crack player, and a most interesting personality, and so was his cousin, a professor in a great eastern university. John Tresevant, as he placed his ball and took his stance, had a feeling that he had a mental reprieve, and might enjoy himself at least for the morning. After lunch he certainly must excuse himself and make those calls briefly, and then lock himself into his study and get to work.

But after lunch the rest of the foursome were keen for another eighteen holes. They liked the handsome young preacher with his sure strokes and his witty tongue. Tresevent said he really must go, and described the distresses of his various parishioners briefly. But Elliot Rand gave him a look that flung all his excuses to the winds. He mimicked each of the poor and distressed most laughably, and practically required his presence for the afternoon.

"It is most important, my dear fellow!" he said in a low tone with a persuasive hand on Tresevant's arm, and a look that made it quite impossible to get away.

The sun was beginning to send long slant rays across the smooth greens, when John Tresevant, triumphant, with an enviably low score, and fresh from a swim in the pool and a shower, met the ladies of the party who had been having their own game of bridge on the wide veranda of the club house. He intended to partake of the delicious lemonade and then hurry away to his belated work.

"And now, Tresevant," said Elliot Rand cheerfully as they settled down in the comfortable rockers to sip their cold drink, "we've decided to make a day of it and all drive up the mountain and have dinner together. You needn't begin to make excuses again. I have it all fixed up. You see you are known to have gone away with me for your vacation, and not a half dozen of the flock will realize that you are home. Your vacation doesn't end anyway until midnight tonight and I intend personally to see that you get every fraction of a second of the time. Besides, my friend Clinton here wants to talk something over with you. He has an idea about those windows if he decides to arrange for it, and it is really imperative that you tell him your wishes concerning coloring and subjects, you know. I tried to sketch your plan to him, but I couldn't remember everything you said, and I want you to talk with him. We're bringing him back for the midnight train, and there won't be any other time, as he's sailing for Europe next week."

"Why, I could send you over the list of subjects," said the young minister politely, "but I really don't see how I could possibly spare the evening. I have no preparation for tomorrow—"

"That's all right, Tresevant," said Elliot Rand with a laughing wave of the hand, "we'll excuse you from being intellectual tomorrow. No preacher tries to do much in the pulpit the first Sunday after his vacation. And you know there won't be anybody out that matters anyway. They haven't come back from their vacations yet."

Tresevant drew his brows as he sipped his drink, and tried to puzzle it out. How was he going to do all that was required of him and yet take in this new delightful interlude?

And even as he thought, his host was again planning his way for him, as he had been doing for the past two weeks, just a downy bed of ease to rest his luxurious soul upon.

"He has plenty of old sermons, hasn't he, Mrs. Tresevant?" Elliot Rand was saying to Elaine.

"Why, of course!" she acquiesced. "They're all over the place and he won't let me clear them up and put them away. And just the day before we went away there arrived a whole big cabinet full of his earlier sermons. I'm sure he hasn't ever tried them on this church at all, for they've been stored at his father's house in New England."

"There!" cried Elliot Rand, "that settles it! We

won't take no for an answer. Seriously, Tresevant, I ask this as a special favor!"

Elliot Rand fixed his fine eyes on the minister's face and smiled one of those cocksure smiles. Tresevant knew he must give in, or break with this man who took it so for granted that he owned him; and such a break would be a more serious matter than he was prepared to make on so short a notice.

Suddenly Tresevant put down his half-finished glass on the table beside him and rose to his feet.

"That being the case," he said gravely, almost haughtily, "I shall have to leave you at once and go to the hospital before I can possibly go anywhere else. I promised Mrs. Addison—"

"Oh—is Addison one of those on your list? Well, of course, you could stop there on the way. It ought not to take you long. He may not even be living. They told me this morning he hadn't a chance."

"You knew that this morning?" asked the minister with a startled look at his host. Then he turned quickly and started down the steps toward the hospital not far away. There were times when John Tresevant could be very decisive indeed, and now it had suddenly come over him what it would mean if this prominent man in his church should die without his attendance, and it should be found out that he had been playing golf nearby all day!

"We'll pick you up in ten minutes!" shouted Rand.

"Poor John! He's always so conscientious!" sighed Elaine prettily.

The men watched him thoughtfully.

"A most interesting man, your husband, Mrs.

Tresevant," observed the elder Mr. Clinton, the one with the money to invest for eternity.

Fifteen minutes later two cars drew up in front of the hospital and waited ten minutes more before the minister came down with a troubled look.

"I think you'll have to count me out!" he said decisively to Elliot Rand. "There are several other people I ought to see, and I really should get back to my study."

"Nonsense!" said that demogogue sharply. "Get in! We've waited long enough! Did you find Mr. Addison still living?"

"Yes, but unconscious. He is very near the end. I was there in time to offer a prayer. I think his wife would never have forgiven me if he had passed on without it, and—" he added thoughtfully, "I'm afraid I should never have forgiven myself."

"Oh, for pity's sake, John! How silly! What possible good could a prayer do, even if the man was conscious to hear it?" said Elaine contemptuously.

"Get in," said Elliot Rand again, this time with authority. "If you have to go anywhere else this evening, we're taking you, and making sure of you."

He held the door open for the minister and Tresevant got hesitantly into the car.

"I must go to Hargraves' to see about the funeral," he said, "and I must see Mr. Barker. His wife has been taken to the asylum and he wants me; and I should go to Mrs. Brown!"

"Nonsense!" said Elliot Rand sternly. "The Hargraves funeral can be arranged in the morning. You can telephone from the Mountain House that you expect to arrive home about midnight and will be over the first thing in the morning. As for Mr. Barker, there's no rush about him. I've known him a good many years and this isn't the first time his wife has been taken to the asylum. And Mrs. Brown has a broken leg and can't get up and leave the church tonight, so you are safe. You'll find your call just as acceptable tomorrow afternoon. No, forget it, parson, and let's have a good time. We've got you, and we mean to keep you!"

But John Tresevant sat unsmiling in his seat, looking troubled. It was not only that he had just been in the hovering presence of death. It was not wholly that he knew the prayer he had just uttered was nothing but empty words, hurrying to be finished before the soul passed out of this world, that he might not be counted to have failed in his duty toward this prominent man. It was that he felt shamed. All day he had been racing after a good time to please others, with his conscience prodding him and reminding him that it was all wrong, the kind of life he was living.

As he settled back in the luxurious car and was rushed through the city and out into the far reaches of lovely country road, by clear winding rivers and towering rocks, through picturesque villages, with the hazy blue of a distant mountain for a goal, and a spirit of gaiety around him, somehow he seemed to be set apart from his companions. No longer could he forget his duty, and the oncoming services, for which he was not prepared, and enter into the good cheer of the hour. He was distraught and silent, tired and worried. He realized that he would have to sit up all night to get ready for his morning's sermon. He must somehow think out a theme, with an outline. That was the trouble with having set the standard of fine preaching in the past. He must keep it up. He could not have them saying that he was not preaching as interesting sermons as formerly.

Elliot Rand might tell him that it didn't matter what he preached, but he would not hesitate to criticize afterward. Tresevant knew by sorry experience.

But there was little time to meditate on sermons. He was seated next to Mr. Clinton who began a rapid fire of questions about the new church.

Then they were at the beautiful hotel before they realized and spent a long time over the excellent dinner that was served to them.

But at last it was time to start home. They chose a different way to return because it was supposed to be shorter and the hour was late.

They sped over the road at a good pace, until suddenly they came to a halt so abruptly that it almost threw the whole company upon their knees. The car behind belonging to the young professor barely swerved in time to avoid a dangerous collision.

The road ahead was partly shut off and marked with red lanterns. A sign announced that travelers would proceed at their own risk, as the road was under repair.

The men of the party got out and consulted, even walking down the road under question for some distance. They finally decided to risk it, as they had come more than halfway. They could not possibly get Mr. Clinton to his train if they went back by the other road, for there was no cross cut to it.

But the road grew worse and worse. In places it was corrugated and sent the travelers up in the air and down again with uneven rhythm, like a gigantic rocking horse. They groaned and laughed about it at first, but when this continued for several miles they grew silent and cross. There were no signs anywhere, and the moon had withdrawn behind an ominous cloud.

Then suddenly the leading car lurched and reeled, there was a grinding sound, and they came to a standstill at a fearful angle, with two of the wheels down in a gully of soft thick mud.

The men got out again to investigate, shaking their heads gravely. Then each with a desperate look at his shoes and his good clothes, stepped down into what seemed a fathomless abyss, and pitted his strength against the mammoth bulk of machinery that lolled in the muck and darkness. Tresevant was no shirker, and before many minutes his white flannels which had remained immaculate during the long, delightful day, were smeared beyond recognition with mud and grease.

Desisting at last from the impossible task of straightening up the car, Tresevant and the professor decided to walk up the mountain after assistance.

But it was hours later that a sadder and a wiser company of holiday makers were finally dragged up the mountain to a service station for repairs.

The minister grimly stood in the shadows at the side of the road and stared into the darkness while they waited for repairs. He was too weary to think, but he *must* decide what to do about a sermon.

The morning was about to dawn when at last the two cars got underway and started back to the road they had driven up so happily that afternoon.

They dropped the minister at his own door just as the milkman was going his morning rounds. But scarcely had Tresevant put the key in the lock of his front door before a car whirled up to the curb, and the Addison chauffeur came hurrying up the walk.

"Mr. Tresevant," he said respectfully, "Mrs. Addison says will you come right over to the hospital at once! Mr. Addison has rallied and is asking for you."

Tresevant looked down at his shoes and his smudged white flannels in dismay, yet he knew he must go.

"Oh, *John!* You must have some breakfast first!" said Elaine firmly.

"I was told to say that Mr. Addison may pass away at any moment, ma'am!" said the chauffeur, and there was almost contempt in the look he gave her.

"I'll be right with you," said Tresevant, tearing up the stairs three steps to a stride.

He climbed out of the soiled white flannels and muddy shoes and into his serge suit with a single movement as it were, made the gesture of washing his face, and combed his hair with a pocket comb on the way downstairs.

"John! You *mustn't!* You really *mustn't!*" called Elaine futilely.

Mr. Addison died a half-hour later, but Tresevant had gone through the form of another prayer with him, and Mrs. Addison was duly grateful. The Addison car delivered him at the manse again just as Elaine was coming down to breakfast. But the minister hadn't had time even to taste his coffee before the telephone rang.

"It's the Hargraves, sir," said the maid. "They say they must wire the married son about the funeral, and could you come over at once?"

Tresevant gulped a few swallows of coffee and went out again, amid more protests from Elaine, who had much to say about the trials of a minister's *wife*.

It was almost half past ten when the minister got back from Hargraves' and there was no sermon as yet!

Tresevant tore into his study and began to fling neat manuscripts about wildly. There on his desk lay his effort of yesterday morning smiling up at him in clear fair script: "The trouble with the world today is—"

If he could only get hold of the thread of his theme! But to save him all he could think of that the world needed just now was some sleep.

Elaine was standing in the doorway smiling at him, fresh as a rose in her lovely fall costume.

"Where is that case of sermons you said came from home?" he yelled fiercely.

"Right over there in the corner, dearest!" she said sweetly. "But they're not open. You couldn't possibly get them open now. And you must go and put on a clean shirt and a necktie! Why, John! That's your old suit you have on! You'll *have* to change! And there! The second bell is ringing! Why not just give them a little talk about that lovely sunset we saw at sea last week. You can do it wonderfully, you know."

"Where is the axe? I ask you? Where is the axe, or a hatchet? Or even a hammer and screwdriver? Isn't there a tool of any sort around the house *ever?*" His tone was rising far above the ordinary ministerial modulation, and the maid appeared at the door with the axe.

The minister grasped it and went for the sermon case as though it were an enemy threatening the life of his family. *Crash!* came down the axe on the stubborn wood. *Crash!*

"John! What will the people going by think at hearing such sounds from the manse on Sunday morning?"

Crash!

"I don't care what they think!" said the minister.

"John! You will ruin that lovely mahogany cabinet inside. Why will you be so silly? You can't possibly hunt a sermon now. John! I only sent for that because I wanted that lovely cabinet for my music, and now you're ruining it!"

Crash!

"I'll be ruined myself if I can't find a sermon," said the minister, bringing down his axe ruthlessly and splintering the outer box with fervor.

Another crash or two and the box was conquered,

and simultaneously the cabinet door sprang open, letting out an avalanche of manuscripts in neat brown paper covers.

The minister pounced upon one almost gleefully. It looked familiar and gave him comfort. At least it was *some*thing. If it didn't suit the high and mighty Elliot Rand it was his own fault, and he would tell him so when he came around to criticize.

With a deep drawn breath, something like a sigh of relief, the minister caressed the sermon, and turned wildly toward the door, as the last stroke of the second bell sounded melodiously on the air.

"John! You're *not* going to church that way! You've got a smudge on your nose, and your hair looks like a haystack!" screamed his wife as he tore out the manse door and across the lawn to the church.

But John Tresevant strode on.

In the church study the elders were gathering for the formality of a prayer before the service, a ceremony instituted by a former pastor and insisted upon by an old-fashioned senior elder.

Tresevant knelt beside his chair and signed to the senior elder to pray. He reflected that he would have time to glance at the heading of his sermon during the singing, and find out what Scripture would be appropriate to read for it. He had always been so particular about writing down those little details when he first began his ministry.

"Lord, we pray thee that thou wilt be with our beloved pastor today and endue him with power from on high! *Help him,* Lord, that we may through his message behold Jesus, our Savior!"

The words were so typical of the senior elder that at any other time they would have passed the minister's preoccupied mind unaware, but suddenly they took life and rang in his ears. Help! That was what he needed! Help! How he used to cry to God for help in those early days. How uncertain he used to be of himself, and how dependent upon God! How he *used* to get almost in a panic before he went into the pulpit, lest he would fail, and bring dishonor upon his Lord! He almost smiled as he remembered. For now he was so certain of himself—usually. He used to say that he must spend as much time in prayer as he spent in study or his message was a failure. Now his prayers were wild and hurried and desultory, with his mind upon the unique and arresting sentences with which his discourse was to open.

Suddenly he realized that he was in a worse panic now than he had ever been in his life before. His brain was empty and his mind was in a whirl. He had nothing, absolutely nothing, between him and disaster but that little brown-paper-covered sermon in his hand.

"God! Help me! Give me a message! God! God! Where are you? Can't you hear me anymore?"

It was all in his heart, this wild cry. The senior elder had brought his prayer to a close and given place to the one next in authority, a little man with a thin, unconvincing voice who was droning out a list of requests.

But Tresevant did not hear them. Suddenly it was the Lord Himself who was standing there in his study, looking down upon him. He could feel His hand laid upon his head, and His voice was as clear in his heart as words spoken.

"John Tresevant," he said, "you and I used to walk together. Do you remember that? You and I died together on the cross years ago. Have you forgotten that? In those days when we walked together I could give you my messages, and you could carry them to souls that needed them, but you have walked strange paths of late, paths where I could not go, and you have been so far away from me that you could not hear my voice. Even when you asked for help you did not come near enough to get it. You are too far away this morning. You do not really want my help. You think you are smart enough to do this thing yourself, so you will have to do it alone. I cannot help you till you are ready to walk with me again, and can hear my voice. You will have to do the best you can!"

The prayers around the minister suddenly ceased. He mumbled a few words of formal closing and arose, his face white and drawn, and went unsmiling, unseeing, into his pulpit, the little old brown-paper-covered sermon clutched in his hand, the only connection between himself and a deserted God.

He found the place in the Bible, the Scripture he was to read, but he was suddenly faced with the realization that next in order was the long prayer, and praying meant addressing the God who had just spoken to his heart back there in the study, who had rebuked him for not walking with Him! And what could he say to a God who had separated Himself from him?

Down there in the audience sat Elliot Rand, with Mr. Clinton and the professor. Yesterday Elliot Rand had laughingly boasted about what wonderful prayers his minister made, comparing them to a beautiful embroidery of words. That was what was expected of him now, to embroider a prayer for the delicate ears of his congregation, a prayer that should be a fitting accompaniment to, and perhaps suggest, the mellow light of costly windows in a new edifice. And suddenly John Tresevant was afraid of God, the God whom he, as the mouthpiece of a large audience, must approach in prayer.

Back in the early days of his ministry, when his heart was on fire for God, when his whole being was filled with a zeal for soul-winning, and his consciousness was always permeated with the sense of the presence of God, his prayers vibrated with love. Praying had been like coming to a loving Father, knowing that what he asked would be granted because he and his Father were of one accord. It flashed upon him now that he had lost this close fellowship with God, that the prayer he was about to make was a counterfeit, a mere display of words.

He opened his lips to speak and the Lord stood there before him, looking into his soul again with that searching gaze. The Lord, with his pierced hands and his wounded side and the look of hurt love in his eyes. And suddenly Tresevant's flow of gracious words was cut off, and he had nothing wherewith to cry out to God but the humble, contemptible confessions of a sinner!

He forgot to pray for "the president and officers of these United States," and "for those in authority." He forgot to pray for those on foreign fields carrying the message, forgot the sick and suffering, the sad and fearful, and prayed only for mercy! And yet such was the sincerity of his prayer that somehow every man, woman, and child in the audience was made to feel his own need of mercy, and that the prayer was especially for him.

It was very still in the room while he was praying, and when the petition was ended more than one in the audience was wiping his eyes.

But Tresevant was not watching his audience. He was conscious only of that Presence that was standing in his pulpit with him. The Presence that during the first two years of his ministry had been with him always when he preached. Then his message had been given to please his Lord and not his congregation.

Where had that Presence been? Why had he lost the sense of his nearness? *When* had he lost it? He tried to think back. Did it begin about the time when he first met Elaine, the lovely girl who had seemed so far above him socially, financially, and yet so desirable, so angelic? Had he wandered away from the Lord to please Elaine? And now to please his congregation? Elliot Rand?

These thoughts like accusing persons seemed to flock around him and hide his congregation from his view, as he sat down in the great pulpit chair and shaded his eyes with his hand while the costly organ swelled forth the hymn, and the people, led by the well-trained choir, sang.

Tresevant did not hear his congregation singing.

"God," he was saying behind his sheltering hand, "O God, I can't do it. I'm going to break down. I've never broken down, but now I'm done. You'll have to help me. My strength and my assurance are gone!"

Elaine watched him with startled, annoyed eyes as he rose with white stricken face to read the Scripture. So silly for him to think he had to go out to those clamoring parishioners when he so needed sleep!

It was the thirty-eighth Psalm that the sermon had called for, and suddenly as he glanced at its heading Tresevant recalled it and it seemed the very cry of his own soul. Unconsciously he read aloud the notes he had carefully printed in the margin of his Bible, put there long ago when the great truths first gripped him.

" 'This Psalm is the cry of a saved soul under conviction of sin.' Its heading in our Bibles reads: A psalm of David, *to bring to remembrance!* It reminds us of Paul's words in the New Testament: 'If we would judge ourselves we would not be judged!' "

The minister paused as the crushing truths broke upon his own soul. The congregation was breathless. Then slowly he read, as if he had forgotten the people, as if he were crying out himself to that Presence there before him in the pulpit.

"O Lord, rebuke me not in thy wrath; neither chasten me in thy hot displeasure. There is no soundness in my flesh because of thine anger; neither is there any rest in my bones because of my sin. For mine iniquities are gone over my head; as a heavy burden they are too heavy for me—" his voice broke and he brought out his confession clearly, "because of—my—*foolishness!*"

A sob almost broke through the huskiness of the minister's voice. The audience was tensely still. Elliot Rand was listening in horrified, incredulous contempt, but the man standing before his God neither saw nor cared.

On he read through the verses that followed, even reading aloud his interpolated notes.

" 'Lord . . . my groaning is not hid from thee . . .'—the cry of a soul in anguish. 'In thee, O Lord, do I hope . . .' Confession of sin at last: 'For I will declare my iniquity; I will be sorry for my sin. . . . Forsake me not, O Lord. O my God be not far from me. Make haste to help me, O Lord my salvation.' "

As Tresevant finished reading and sat down, the hush was instantly filled with soft organ tones and the choir broke forth into lovely music as if to soothe the minds so strangely stirred, and cause them to forget the ugly words about *sin.*

Tresevant was clutching that sermon that he must now preach. In the light of that chapter he had just read he must get up and preach!

And now he knew which sermon this was that he held in his hand. It was one that had been written almost upon his knees, and it had never been delivered except after much prayer. He had always gone to deliver it as to a sacred trust, gone with his face shining from communion with his Lord. And that sermon had always brought fruit for Christ.

But that was a long time ago, when he walked with his God. That was before he knew Elaine, or Elliot Rand; when he had a plain little church with a congregation that was hungry for the word of truth.

Now he was standing in a worldly congregation where he had many times smothered the truth in pretty phrases. Now his sin of estrangement had come between his Lord and himself and it seemed to him that the message was no longer his to give.

He arose and stood staring down at the words. It was then that he suddenly realized that the opening sentence of this sermon was identical with the one he had started on Saturday morning:

"The trouble with the world today is—"

Of course he hadn't been able to finish it then. He hadn't known then what was the trouble with the world. *Now* he knew!

"The trouble with the world today is that it has lost its sense of sin, and of its awful need of a Savior!"

The startled congregation, already deeply stirred by the unusual prayer and Scripture reading, sat up and stared at him.

But Tresevant went on setting forth great truths, the old familiar sentences sweeping to his lips.

"Men today are unwilling to admit their sin because that would hurt their pride. It is a humbling thing to confess sin! Men are provoked when God discounts all of their self-righteousnesses and calls them filthy rags!"

Elliot Rand was beginning to get angry. Two red spots appeared on his cheeks. Was his prince of a preacher going fanatical on him?

Elaine stared at her husband contemptuously. Was this really John Tresevant daring to give voice to such outworn puritanical dogmas? What would people think?

But the people were weeping and listening breathlessly.

"Men are playing with life today," said Tresevant earnestly, "and God is waiting, watching, searching hearts! Looking with longing eyes at his redeemed ones, those of us who have named his name, and accepted him as our Savior, and have started out—to—witness—for him—"

Suddenly Tresevant paused, his voice broke, he bent his head an instant, drawing a deep breath. Then lifting his haggard face he tried once more to go on with husky broken voice, but the words halted upon his lips and he closed his eyes. Then looking up he said in a low tragic tone:

"I am not worthy. *I* have sinned! I cannot go on!"

He turned back to his pulpit chair and sank into it with his face in his hands.

There was an awful moment of silence during which it seemed that heaven and hell were awaiting the outcome, and God stood there in the pulpit with condemning eyes looking at them all.

Then suddenly a voice at the back of the church began to pray. It was the old senior elder whom nobody ever reckoned of any account.

"O our God, *all* we like sheep have gone astray,

we have turned every one to his own way, but thou hast laid upon thy Son the iniquity of us all. We thank thee for the Lord Jesus today, for we have seen *him*, hanging on the cross for us, bearing the cruel penalty of our sins, taking punishment by punishment all that was meant for us, all that was by right our score to settle. We have seen what he has done for us, and in the presence of his glory and his grace we have seen as in a mirror, our own silly, sinful selves, groveling here after the tinsel and toys put out by the enemy of our souls to decoy us from life and eternal joy with thee. O Lord, we thank thee for this vision of ourselves, and for the vision of thee we have had today. We have for a long time been longing for this, and we thank thee that today thou hast given to the earthly shepherd of our souls this message for us. So we confess our guilt and come to thee for cleansing—"

Suddenly there was a little stir in the center of the church and Elliot Rand, followed by the Clintons, stalked silently down the aisle and left the church. And Elaine with a frightened furtive glance at her husband, slipped out as silently as a shadow.

Then, as if the enemy had gone out like a troop, the Spirit of the Lord seemed suddenly to descend upon that gathering, as one after another of the members of the church took up the prayer of the old Scotch elder, till prayer had swept like a heavenly fire about that room. Prayer laden with confession of sin. Prayer for the pastor and for the church. Prayer for the town.

They lingered a long time afterward, asking forgiveness of one another, telling their pastor how he had searched their hearts, how they had been helped and blessed, shaking his hand with deep feeling, with tears, urging him to preach like that all the time, blessing the Lord for sending him.

But when at last John Tresevant went slowly out the door with the old Scotch elder by his side, he saw standing by the curb the luxurious limousine in which he had gone holidaying yesterday, and by it stood his wife and Elliot Rand talking most earnestly together.

They met him with strange, forced, alien smiles.

"Get in, Tresevant," said Elliot Rand kindly, as one might talk to a sick child. "We are taking you somewhere to rest."

The minister turned and looked at his erstwhile friend and host. There was a strange new light in his eyes that Elliot Rand did not know.

"To rest?" he said. "I don't need rest. I have just got back to the resting place of my soul!" and there was a new ring to his voice that Elliot Rand had never heard.

"Yes?" said Elliot Rand. "Well, get in, please. We are going to take you to a lovely place where your body may have rest, too. You needn't stop to explain to the congregation. I'll attend to all that. Just get in and lie back and rest. I feel that we owe you a great apology for keeping you on such a long strain all night."

There was a light in Tresevant's eyes as he faced Elliot Rand.

"Oh, *that?*" he said. "I'd forgotten about the night.

That was nothing! It is good of you of course to try to plan for me, but I haven't time now to go anywhere to rest. I've found my Lord and I intend never to leave him again. Tonight's service is coming, and I must find out what my Lord would have me do about it. Good-bye." And he turned and walked across the lawn to the manse.

"John!" cried his wife in dismay. But he did not seem to hear her.

A few minutes later she burst into his study, an angry spot of color on each cheek, and fire in her eyes.

"Well, just what do you think you are doing now?" she demanded as she entered. "Are you trying to make me ashamed that I ever married you, or have you lost your mind, or what? I never saw such an exhibition in all my life! A nice way to treat Elliot Rand after all he's done for you!"

And then she stopped, for she saw her husband was on his knees beside his desk praying.

He glanced up and there was such a look of radiance upon his face that she stepped back in a kind of awe. She had not seen that look on his face in a long, long time.